The Multi-Church Parish

Creative Leadership Series

The Multi-Church Parish

Robert L. Wilson

Creative Leadership Series

Lyle E. Schaller, Editor

Abingdon Press / Nashville

THE MULTI-CHURCH PARISH

Copyright © 1989 by Abingdon Press

This book is printed on acid-free paper.

Library of Congress Cataloging-in-Publication Data

Wilson, Robert Leroy, 1925–
  The multi-church parish / Robert L. Wilson.
    p. cm. — (Creative leadership series)
  Bibliography: p.
  ISBN 0-687-27290-4
  1. Larger parishes. I. Title. II. Series.
BV638.4.W55   1989
254—dc20

89-32531
CIP

MANUFACTURED BY THE PARTHENON PRESS AT
NASHVILLE, TENNESSEE, UNITED STATES OF AMERICA

To Betty,
whose support and assistance
made this book possible

Contents

Foreword

Do we have an oversupply of clergy or are we short of pastors? That is a question high on the agenda of many denominational leaders, as well as a big issue facing scores of theological seminaries.

What is the appropriate role for that growing number of mature Christians who feel a call to the ministry late in life? Should they be encouraged to go to seminary or should they be advised it is too late, that perhaps God spoke to them earlier, but they did not hear the call?

How should we respond to the fact that the Consumer Price Index, which stood at 27 in 1906, has now passed 380 (1967-100), an increase of about fourteen times the 1906 figure in less than eighty-five years, but the average compensation for pastors is now more than twenty times what it was in 1906? How do we respond, as congregations who must pay the salaries of those pastors, to that fact of life?

The usual approach is to appoint a special committee to study a difficult question and to return with recommendations for future consideration. A better approach may be to look first at the larger situation before turning to a detailed examination of a particular problem. That is one among five reasons for asking someone to write a book such as this one.

The primary audience for this book consists of ministers

who have been asked to serve a multi-church parish. Many of them grew up in an urban or suburban setting, attended a relatively large church, graduated from a college or university located in a metropolitan community, and chose an urban seminary for their theological studies. Placement in a rural multi-church parish naturally produced a sense of discontinuity. This is a completely new experience! Where do I begin? How do I understand the dynamics of this arrangement? What are the expectations people have of their minister? One answer is, read this book!

A second audience is the lay leadership of those congregations that share a minister with another church. This book is intended to help them understand the complexity of these arrangements with a touch of realism, especially as they welcome a new minister who has had no prior experience with a multi-church parish.

A third audience consists of those denominational executives who find that their regional judicatory includes several multi-church parishes. Again, many of these leaders had no firsthand experience with this concept before coming into their present position. Most of them were pastors of larger churches and the role of serving as the pastor of a multi-church parish is not a part of their prior experience. These leaders will find this to be an immensely helpful and practical guide to many of the intricacies of these arrangements.

The fourth audience may strike some as the most obvious. This book is also for use in those theological seminaries from which many graduates go directly to serve as the pastor of a multi-church parish. Dozens of seminaries report that at least one-fourth of the graduates who go directly into the parish ministry find their first assignment to be a multi-church parish.

The fifth audience overlaps the other four, but is really composed of those leaders who want a larger context for examining specific issues. This book provides that larger context for many questions. This can be illustrated by looking at ten frequently raised issues.

1. How do we provide ministerial leadership for those thousands of smaller congregations that cannot afford or justify a full-time resident pastor? At least a dozen answers can be offered to that question. (See Lyle E. Schaller, *The Small Church Is Different!* pp. 84-108.) One of them is the multi-church parish. This book offers a detailed analysis of that alternative.

2. How do we respond to the fact that the total compensation for a full-time minister has continued to climb and thus has priced a growing number of congregations out of the ministerial marketplace?

One response has been to encourage two or three congregations to share the services of one minister and thus be able to obtain a full-time pastor. This book provides the material for an evaluation of that option.

3. Should we encourage our smaller congregations to come together in some form of a cooperative ministry?

Chapter 7 provides a detailed and realistic analysis of a common approach to cooperative ministries. The author has removed the romantic veneer that has frightened off some critics and explains both the attractive features and the limitations of this concept.

4. Do we have an oversupply of clergy or are we facing a shortage of pastors in the years ahead?

One of the reasons behind the dissolution of multi-church parishes has been an effort to provide more jobs for seminary graduates. If one assumes that an average attendance of one hundred or more at worship is needed to both justify and support a full-time resident pastor who has no other employment, it is clear we are confronted with an excess of ministers. Fewer than 40 percent of the 375,000 Protestant congregations in the United States and Canada average at least one hundred in worship.

The United Methodist Church, for example, includes

fewer than 12,000 congregations that average one hundred or more at worship, but has 23,000 ministers serving churches and who are guaranteed appointments at or above minimum salary. One means of responding to the current surplus of clergy is to encourage the formation of multi-church parishes "to make a salary." Another is to urge the breakup of these arrangements in order to create a need for more ministers.

This book offers a larger context for choosing between those alternatives.

5. How do we respond to the growing call for a greater emphasis on the ministry of the laity?

One option is to encourage those thousands of congregations with fewer than thirty-five or forty at worship to transform themselves into lay led religious communities. A second is the bi-vocational pastor, typically a layperson who serves one church on a part-time basis. A third is to encourage a greater role for the laity by encouraging those arrangements where one minister serves as the pastor of two to ten congregations with a group of volunteer colleagues drawn from among the laity.

This book offers a larger context for examining these and other alternatives.

6. Where can we place that rapidly growing number of laypeople who respond late in life to a call to the ministry of Word and Sacrament?

If a surplus of clergy already exists, what opportunities are open to the fifty-three-year-old seminary graduate? One answer is, they often receive a very warm welcome as the new pastor of the multi-church parish.

7. How do we respond to the fact that while in general the size of churches is increasing, in our denomination the average size is going down?

One aspect of that issue is the growing number of congregations that average more than two thousand persons at worship on Sunday morning. That number has at least quadrupled since 1955 and may even be ten times what it was as recently as 1949.

A second aspect of that picture is that the average (mean) size of all Christian congregations on this continent has at least tripled since 1900.

The third, and to many the most disturbing aspect of this subject is that while in general congregations are growing larger, in several denominations the average (mean) size is shrinking. This is illustrated by the figures for the eight oldline Protestant denominations shown in the accompanying table. The average size of an Episcopal parish has dropped by nearly 60 communicant members—from 317 in 1968 to 258 in 1986. For three of the eight denominations, the decrease is a double digit number in only eighteen years.

Average* Size of Congregations

	1968	1986
American Lutheran Church	362	355
Christian Church (Disciples of Christ)	272	265
Episcopal Church	317	258
Lutheran Church in America	374	370
Presbyterian Church in the U.S.A.	330**	263
Presbyterian Church in Canada	174	157
United Church of Christ	296	263
United Methodist Church	262**	240

*This is the mean based on confirmed membership.
**Combined figures for predecessor denominations.

One response to that trend is the subject of this book, to encourage more congregations to consider the multi-church parish as a means of securing full-time pastoral leadership.

8. Should we discourage multi-church parishes and seek instead to encourage smaller congregations to merge?

This was a popular response back in the 1960s and early 1970s when congregational mergers were seen as the way to produce a middle-sized congregation. In the vast majority of mergers, the key lesson to be learned was that two plus two often equals two, and sometimes three, but rarely four or five. A few of the reasons for this can be found in chapter 8—and also why the concept of multi-church parishes may outlive the dream of mergers.

9. Is it realistic to expect smaller churches to grow in numbers? Or is it more realistic to encourage these smaller congregations to seek an arrangement that will produce stability rather than growth?

The historical record makes clear that the basic tendency of the vast majority of smaller congregations is either to remain on a plateau in size or to experience a gradual erosion in numbers.

This book makes clear that numerical growth and multi-church parishes rarely go together. Professor Wilson's analysis can be a useful background to this debate over stability versus growth.

10. Should we encourage growth in the number of bi-vocational pastors? Or should we encourage local church leaders to choose the arrangement which provides a full-time pastor for two or more congregations?

For many readers this is the most challenging and the most pressing of these ten policy questions. Recent years have witnessed a dramatic increase in the number of Christians on this continent who are seeking the opportunity of serving as the pastor of a worshiping community while continuing to spend considerable time in another role. One reason obviously behind this trend is the short work week. A second is the increasing number of smaller congregations. A third is the rapid growth in the number of seminary graduates who want to combine the roles of wife, mother, homemaker, and pastor. A fourth is the sharp increase in the number of mature adults who are accepting a call to the parish ministry,

14

but do not want to leave that secular job. A fifth is the increasing number of people who retire from the labor force before their sixtieth birthday. A sixth is the increasing availability of seminary training off campus. A seventh is the change in the requirements and expectations of several denominations from opposition to tentmakers to a more sympathetic view of the contributions of bi-vocational ministers and dual-role pastors.

This book also offers a useful context for anyone interested in that already.

This is but one of several volumes in the Creative Leadership Series written for the use of leaders concerned with the future of the more than 200,000 small Protestant congregations scattered across the North American continent.

Lyle E. Schaller
Yokefellow Institute
Richmond, Indiana

Introduction

"I love my four churches; the people are great. I'm now working with several lay speakers, so we have services in each church every Sunday. Recently I took a group of senior citizens on a bus tour to Niagara Falls." These comments were made by Vivian, who had been pastor of four rural churches for five years since graduating from seminary. She was a widow in her mid-forties who had been a schoolteacher when she decided to enter the ministry.

"I guess I would say I'm happy here. The people have been supportive and they love their church, but neither of these congregations is going to grow. The population of this county has been declining for about thirty years. This parish is a good place to begin one's ministry." George, the minister who made these remarks, was completing his second year as pastor of two rural congregations. It was his first call since graduating from seminary.

The finance committee was preparing the Walnut Grove Church budget for the coming year. Sidney, the chairman, said: "I am concerned about our income over the long term. Our membership has been decreasing and this has affected our income. We must find a way to reduce expenses. When Reverend Fleming retires at the end of the year we might arrange to have the pastor of Mt. Bethel also serve our church."

Several leaders of Trinity Church were discussing the congregation's future. "We took in eleven new families in the past year," said Ed, the board chairman. "The new factory will bring in more people when it is completed. We will soon be at the point where we can have our own pastor. We've shared a minister with the Willow Creek church for as long as I can remember. It's time we thought about going on our own."

The multi-church parish in which one pastor serves two or more churches has long been and will continue to be a prominent feature of American Protestantism. For many congregations this form of organization is a matter of financial necessity. There are a very large number of small-membership churches that simply do not have the resources to employ a minister. In order to obtain pastoral leadership, such churches must employ someone on a part-time basis. This means having a bi-vocational minister—that is, someone who holds a secular job in addition to serving as pastor of a church—or obtaining the services of a retired minister or a semi-retired former military chaplain. Such persons can work part time because they are receiving a pension. Churches within commuting distance of a theological seminary may employ students who can spend weekends at the church while attending school during the week.

However, many persons who feel that they have been called to the ministry and have spent seven years in preparation want to devote all their time to being a pastor. In order to do this, many ministers serve multi-church parishes consisting of two or more congregations. This allows the individual to serve full time while enabling many small churches to have an ordained pastor who has met the denomination's educational requirements.

The multi-church parish is deeply rooted in the tradition of

18

certain denominations. This is particularly true of, but not limited to, United Methodists. The circuit has been a vital part of Methodism since its founding. The image of the early years of this denomination is that of the circuit rider making his rounds, preaching, baptizing, and assisting the local non-ordained preachers who cared for the congregation on a day-to-day basis. The circuit riding preacher is epitomized in Francis Asbury, who traveled more than a quarter of a million miles by horseback and did much to establish Methodism in America.

Today, there are literally thousands of congregations throughout the country that share a pastor with two or more other churches. Although the exact number of multi-church parishes is not known, the figure is substantial. A scrutiny of the number of pastors and churches provides a clue to the percentage of congregations sharing a minister. There are probably 50,000 such congregations in America.

Multi-church parishes are found to some degree in virtually every denomination, including Presbyterian, the several branches of Lutheranism, Episcopal, United Church of Christ, American Baptist, and the Christian Church (Disciples of Christ). The percentage of churches that share a pastor ranges from about one in ten in some denominations to about six in ten in others. It is safe to say that a majority of Protestant clergy and a substantial portion of lay members will at some time have experience with a multi-church parish. Furthermore, this situation will continue for the indefinite future.

This book will examine the various aspects of the multi-church parish and address such matters as, how a pastor ministers to more than one church, how congregations relate to one another, ways of devising a workable Sunday schedule, what can and cannot be done on a parish-like basis, who has first claim on the pastor's time, and how financial arrangements are made. This approach is practical. It is hoped that these materials will be of value to both pastors and laypersons as they minister through local churches that are part of a multi-church parish.

The author wishes to express his appreciation to the many persons who made this study possible. These include pastors and lay members in multi-church parishes who provided the data this book is based on. A grant from the Duke Endowment helped fund the research. Valuable insights and critiques were provided by Albert F. Fisher, Director of the Office of Rural Church Affairs of the Duke Endowment; A. Clay Smith, Executive Director of the Hinton Rural Life Center; and colleagues at the Duke Divinity School, particularly M. Wilson Nesbitt. A special word of appreciation is due Candice Y. Sloan, Anne C. Regan, and Ginny W. Ashmore of the J. M. Ormond Center for Research, Planning and Development, who assisted with the research and in the preparation of the manuscript.

Robert L. Wilson
Divinity School
Duke University

I.

The Multi-Church Parish

The multi-church parish has long been a feature of American Protestantism. It is probable that it will be a prominent part of most denominations for the indefinite future. The reason is simple: There are vast numbers of congregations too small to employ a full-time minister and thus they must find a part-time pastor. Many of these churches are in communities not likely to grow, so the church will also continue to remain small. The result is an increasing number of small churches being priced out of the preacher market as clergy compensation rises faster than the congregational receipts. Furthermore, some churches once large enough to afford a full-time minister are shrinking in size and resources.

A large portion of the multi-church parishes are located in rural areas and small towns. It was in such communities that many Protestant churches were established as people settled the frontier. The rural communities have changed in the century since the nation was settled and are continuing to change. The local church is the institution which has changed less. It remains a vital part of the lives of the people. In fact, the church is one of the institutions in the community over which the local people still have a lot of control. The consolidation of farms may have resulted in an area's having a smaller population than it did a generation ago. Businesses may have closed because of a lack of customers. Rail service may long ago have been discontinued, and in some places even the long distance buses no longer operate. The town may have been bypassed by the interstate highway system. The neighborhood school may have been closed and the children bussed to a consolidated school in the county seat. But the people continue to maintain their church by sharing a pastor even though it means that they can have worship services only twice a month.

A substantial number of small membership churches are in urban areas, but few of these are part of a multi-church parish. Small churches in the cities tend to be able to obtain part-time pastoral service without becoming part of a multi-church parish. They have a better opportunity of securing the services of a minister who may also be employed in a church-related institution, have a full-time or part-time secular position, or be a theological student. The number of residents in a city increases the probability that an appropriate part-time pastor can be found for the small city-church.

A Matter of Necessity

The multi-church parish in this period in the life of American Protestantism is an arrangement of convenience or necessity. It is not the choice of the vast majority of either clergy or lay members of small churches, who would prefer that each congregation have its own pastor. The reasons for this are obvious. For the minister, serving two or more congregations is a complex and demanding task. The pastor of a multi-church parish is responsible for two or more congregations, which are not only located in different communities but may also be quite unlike each other. The congregations may or may not get along with each other; there may be some degree of rivalry between them. When asked how his churches get along with each other, one Lutheran pastor replied, "They get along fine in a distant sort of way. They last talked to each other in 1933." Even under the best of circumstances a multitude of details must be worked out so that the programs and the people in the churches of the parish can be adequately cared for. Because the membership of such churches tends to be small, many multi-church parishes can provide only a modest salary. Furthermore, the status of a pastor tends to be related to the size of church he or she serves. The minister serving two or more small congregations will unfortunately be perceived by his or her peers as having a less prestigious position than the person with only one local church.

Most lay members would also prefer not to have to share their pastor with another church or churches although for somewhat different reasons than the ministers. To share a pastor means that the minister must live in a community different from that of at least a portion of the congregation. From time to time there will be scheduling problems, because the events of more than one congregation must be taken into account when congregational activities are planned. Some conflicts are inevitable since the minister is sometimes expected to be in two communities at the same time. Each congregation's share of the joint costs must be agreed on. This can become difficult when one of the churches is much larger than the others making up the parish. It is not uncommon for the congregation that is carrying a major share of the costs to expect first claim on the minister's time when conflicts arise.

Despite the problems, the multi-church parish has enabled many local churches to continue and to have the services of a trained and ordained minister. It has permitted pastors to minister to the residents of rural communities and small towns across the country. Without the multi-church parish, thousands of communities would be without the regular services of an ordained minister. And many rural areas and small towns would be without a resident minister. As one pastor put it, "Having a multi-church parish is an economic decision; it is the only way for many congregations to survive. I could not serve these people if the three churches did not work together."

The Number of Small Churches

Although it is impossible to determine the exact number of multi-church parishes in the different denominations, there is evidence that the number is quite large. Some indication of the total can be determined by examining the number of pastors and the number of churches in the various denominations as reported in *The Yearbook of American and Canadian Churches*.

In most denominations the number of churches exceeds the number of pastors by a substantial margin. For example, the Christian Church (Disciples of Christ) in 1985 had 1,573 more churches than pastors. The American Baptist Church had 1,892 more churches than ministers, the Church of the Nazarene 931, the Presbyterian Church (U.S.A.) 782, the United Church of Christ 1,932, and The United Methodist Church 12,261. Among the major denominations, only the Episcopal Church and the Southern Baptist Convention reported more clergy than local churches.

It does not necessary follow that all the churches in excess of the number of pastors are part of a multi-church parish. Some congregations are served by a part-time pastor. At any given time a number of churches are vacant and in the process of calling a minister. The number of local churches which are part of a multi-church parish varies among denominations. The United Methodists with their long tradition of the circuit riding preacher have large numbers; other communions tend to emphasize one pastor for each congregation and thus have fewer. It can be estimated that in some denominations, such as the Presbyterian Church

(U.S.A.), more than one church in ten shares its pastor, and in others, such as The United Methodist, nearly two out of three congregations are on a circuit. What is clear is that the number of multi-church parishes throughout Protestantism is considerable. A large number of laypeople will continue to share their pastor with one or more other congregations and a large percentage of clergy are likely to serve a multi-church parish during at least a portion of their career.

The Small Church and the Denomination

The small membership churches, many of which are part of a multi-church parish, tend not to conform to the current expectations of what the denomination would like a local church to be and to do. The problem is not primarily that the congregation is part of a multi-church parish but that it is small and therefore cannot meet today's expectations. In a society that places a high value on growth, the small rural church tends to remain the same size. In a society that likes innovation, the small congregation holds to tradition and resists change. In a world where control has become more centralized, the small church continues to assert a high degree of autonomy. In denominations, which are increasingly bureaucratic and complex, the small church continues to be an informal organization where decisions depend on interpersonal and family relationships.

Despite the fact that the total membership of a multi-church parish may be equal to what would be considered a middle-sized town church, it is viewed differently. This is of course because two or three small churches are in fact different from a single congregation of the same number of members. That the large single congregation is perceived as desirable can be attested to by the frequency with which pastors and judicatory officials lament their inability to persuade the churches of a parish to merge and thus form "one good church."

25

The fact is that the small churches are highly valued by the people who worship there and give their time, talent, and resources to keep them open. The likelihood is that many will continue into the future in much the same way they have in the past. They will be served by ministers whom they share with one or more other congregations or by part-time clergy who also hold secular jobs. It therefore places on the lay members, the clergy, and the judicatory officials the responsibility of enabling these churches to be as effective as possible in witnessing to the faith and ministering to the needs of the people.

Organization and the Christian Witness

The Christian witness is made through an institution which we call the church. The church, however, is a collection of institutions with many parts, ranging from a worldwide organization to a group of people in a particular community. The basic unit has always been the local congregation. It is as the local church that the people gather to worship and to hear the Word proclaimed. It is within the setting of the congregation that people become—or fail to become—Christian. The church is of course more than the total number of its congregations. Nevertheless the denominational organization rests on the foundation of its local churches. The health of the denomination with its multitude of institutions and programs depends on the health of its congregations.

Although the local congregation has existed throughout the Christian era, its particular shape and organization have varied widely in different times and in different places. The local church has not only been an expression of the group's theological understanding, it has also reflected the culture of the people. Even congregations of the same denomination will differ from one another as they reflect the subculture of the people of the community in which they are located.

The point is that the gospel can be communicated and the Christian witness made through a range of institutional forms. The form of worship varies and the form of church organization differs, but all appear able to meet the needs of certain groups of people. What is an effective and meaningful form to some people may leave others unaffected.

A particular church may have a small membership because it is located in a sparsely populated community or because its style is the style of congregation the people like. Its small size does not necessarily mean that it is either more or less effective than a congregation of a different size. The Christian church has functioned and will continue to function through a variety of institutional forms.

The multi-church parish is one form of organization small congregations employ to obtain the services of an ordained minister. Like any form of organization, it can range from being very effective to being ineffective. The understanding of the church held by the pastor and people, their willingness to work together, to compromise when conflicts do arise, and their commitment to the task of witnessing and ministering, will ultimately determine the effectiveness of the local church.

II.

What Makes an Effective
Multi-Church Parish

Any consideration of the ways to make a multi-church parish more effective must begin with a realization of two essential facts. The first is that the congregation is the basic unit in the organization of the Christian church. It is the local church which the individual joins and which commands his or her loyalty. The multi-church parish is a cooperative effort of two or more congregations made necessary if each is to have the services of a pastor. The second fact is that every local church is part of a larger community from which it draws its members and with which it is identified.

The multi-church parish is therefore made up of two or more congregations, each of which is a distinct institution with a history, tradition, and identity. The participating congregations are located in different communities, which also have their own distinctiveness. There may be many factors which both the congregations and the communities have in common. The churches which make up the parish will be Lutheran, United Methodist, or Presbyterian and thus share the theological and social heritage of the parent denomination. The communities also may have certain factors in common. They may be rural or consist of small towns; they may have the same economic base. At the same time, each community will have its distinct identity and may perceive the others as rivals. The multi-church parish will be a complex mixture of similarity and diversity.

This chapter will consider the factors that contribute to the effectiveness of the multi-church parish. Most parishes cannot for a variety of reasons be arranged in order to make use of all the factors listed, but the more that are used by a particular parish, the better the chance for increased effectiveness.

Population and Minister's Workload

The congregations and the communities in which they are located must have a sufficient number of people to provide an adequate workload for the minister. Not only must the actual number of resident members be taken into account but also the number of households, which tend to be the giving units. Another important factor is the population trends in the community. If the number of inhabitants is increasing, the congregation will have a better opportunity to grow. If the community is decreasing in population the church membership will have less opportunity to increase. Not only must the potential number of residents be considered but also the types of persons who may be moving into the area. Will the new residents be likely to affiliate with the churches located there? An influx of Roman Catholics does not provide a great opportunity for a Presbyterian church. The long-term population trends will have a significant impact on what the local church is able to do and must be considered when a multi-church parish is contemplated.

An analysis was made of the total number of members in multi-church parishes in seven United Methodist Annual Conferences located in different sections of the country. Twenty-nine percent had fewer than 200 members in all participating churches. Five percent of the multi-church

29

parishes had fewer than 100 members. Many of these are probably served by part-time pastors. Those with between 200 and 400 members accounted for 58 percent of the total. Only 13 percent reported more than 400 members. Given the fact that the pastor is often the only full-time person employed, 200 to 400 members in two or more congregations is generally an adequate workload for clergy in that denomination.

Within The United Methodist Church there is often considerable pressure to subdivide circuits, thereby giving the pastor only one church. Such pressure may come from both the laypersons and the pastor. This can be quite intense if the congregation, though small, is affluent and can afford to pay a full-time salary. Circuits are sometimes divided with the result that the frustration of the pastor and the laypeople is increased. The pastor may have too little to do; the laity may expect the program of the church to expand and the membership to increase. One astute minister in the Midwest was resisting the pressure to divide what he felt was a good two-point circuit. He commented, "If I had only one church instead of two there is little more that I could do except make a few more pastoral calls. The community isn't growing. I'm afraid the people think that not having to share their pastor will make a greater difference than it really can."

Sometimes judicatory officials may support subdividing multi-church parishes to create places for more clergy. In The United Methodist Church the trend in recent years has been for the number of churches to decrease but the number of pastoral appointments to increase. The result is that more ministers are serving fewer congregations than was the case a decade ago. A multi-church parish needs to provide the minister with a challenge which will use his or her abilities. This means a large enough membership not only to have enough people to provide the needed finances, but also enough to give the pastor the opportunity to minister. Without such the pastor may become dispirited and

30

frustrated, and the members may feel burdened by the cost of employing a minister.

Time and Distance

A major factor in determining which congregations can effectively be served by the same pastor is the distance between them and how long it takes to drive from one church to another. The fundamental question is how a minister can effectively serve the several churches located in different communities. If the churches are too far apart, the pastor may have to spend a large amount of time traveling, time that is necessary but also unproductive. A parish begins with already existing congregations and fixed distances, which cannot be changed. Patterns vary greatly in different sections of the country. In the Southeast, with a large rural population, the churches in a parish may be only a few minutes' drive apart. In some sections of the Midwest and Far West, the churches linked in a parish may be many miles and considerable driving time apart.

The distance a pastor must travel between the churches in a parish will determine how he or she relates to the congregations. If the minister can get to each of the churches in 30 to 40 minutes his or her relationship to the churches will be different from that of the minister whose churches are an hour to two hours' drive apart. When the churches are close together, the minister may tend to treat the parish as a unit, often trying to have joint activities. The lay members will perceive the pastor to be readily available. In contrast, churches that are far apart or in separate and unrelated communities tend to encourage good management of time and to discourage the need to have fellowship together just for the sake of cooperation. One pastor, who has served a multi-church parish successfully, observed, "The people recognize that when I'm in one of the other two communities where my churches are located, I'm not available here. They understand my responsibilities to the other churches."

The distance between churches determines the Sunday worship service schedule. Two patterns exist: services each Sunday in two or three churches and services on alternate Sundays in different churches. Where distance permits, the minister conducts two services each week, one in each church. In a few cases, where the churches are sufficiently close together, the pastor will conduct services in three churches. Where the churches are far apart and where there are three or more churches in the parish, services are held on alternate Sundays.

Sometimes the churches are located sufficiently close to permit two or three services, but also far enough apart to make the Sunday morning schedule extremely tight. At the first service the pastor may pronounce the benediction from the rear of the sanctuary and make a mad dash for the car. At the second service a layperson may begin the service which the pastor will join upon arrival. Although such an arrangement is sometimes unavoidable, it is unfortunate. It does not allow the minister time to talk informally with the attenders following the worship service at the first church, the time when much significant communication among church people takes place. Having the pastor rush into a service already in progress is disruptive and not conducive to the most worshipful atmosphere. Whatever distances must be traveled, the churches on the circuit should be located so that the pastor can get from one to another without exceeding the speed limit and still have time to begin the service without being out of breath, even if it means beginning fifteen minutes earlier or concluding fifteen minutes later. Worship is one of the most important events in the life of the church. Every possible step to increase the effectiveness of the Sunday morning worship service should be taken. This is a responsibility which both the laypeople and the pastor must share.

A particular problem exists when a minister has three services on Sunday morning. When there are only two services he or she may arrive early and visit with the people before the first service begins and can remain and visit after the second service ends. When there are three services, however, the pastor may have little or no time either before or after the middle service. Those who serve multi-church parishes tend to be less satisfied with the middle service than with the first or third. Ministers following that schedule may feel they are shortchanging the congregation by not having that highly productive pastoral care time before and after the worship service.

The question is sometimes asked by the clergy and denominational officials why some multi-church parishes do not have the main worship service at a time other than Sunday mornings. A few congregations do, but these are rare. The practice of attending church on Sunday morning is so deeply ingrained in American culture that the likelihood of its being changed is virtually nil.

The Value of Stability

An effective multi-church parish is built on relationships among the congregations and the relationship of the pastor to the different churches. Effective relationships need time to grow. The members of the different churches tend to develop satisfactory ways of adjusting to being a part of a multi-church parish and of working together when they share a pastor for an extended period of time. Patterns of participation in worship services and other church activities are learned. Although the eleven o'clock service continues to be the most popular worship hour, some churches have found other times on Sunday morning equally acceptable. Many farmers prefer an early worship hour. The large church with two services discovers that one group of people tends to prefer to attend the service at nine and a different group at eleven. People get in the habit of worshiping at the same time every week. Pastors and some laypersons in large churches sometimes complain that their church really has two congregations, one that worships at nine and the other at eleven. The patterns of worship attendance represent people's tendency to develop the habit of doing the same thing at the same time each week.

A multi-church parish is more effective if unimportant changes are avoided. From time to time changes must be made, but they should be for valid and important reasons. Superficial alterations that require persons to learn new patterns of behavior should be avoided. Too often a new pastor wants to make changes just to assert his or her authority. These can be disruptive without a corresponding increase in effectiveness.

When a multi-church parish is established it should be with the expectation that it will continue for a very long period of time. A different arrangement should be made only when changes in the community make it essential. If there is a drastic decline in population with a corresponding loss of membership, another church may have to be added to the parish. If the community in which one of the churches is located experiences an increase in population it may be advisable to separate that congregation from the parish to allow the minister to devote his or her time to evangelism and developing programs for the new residents.

There has been a tendency in Protestantism in recent years to become enamored of change. A symptom of this tendency has been the amount of institutional reorganization, which has taken place continually since the mid 1960s. Some changes are, of course, desirable and necessary. But change is always accompanied by some degree of disruption. Planned change, no matter how much careful preparation is done, will have some unforeseen consequences, not all of which will be positive. Local churches and parishes are not immune to the temptation to tinker with the ecclesiastical machinery. To ensure maximum effectiveness, the parish should be allowed to continue with changes instigated only when they are absolutely necessary. The time and energy of the pastor and people could be better used in outreach and program development than in learning new institutional arrangements.

Different patterns can be discerned among the different denominations. Those employing a call system seem to change the parish arrangements less frequently. When asked how long her churches had been served by the same pastor, a Presbyterian responded, "There haven't been any recent changes; the present arrangement was made about 1910." In contrast, The United Methodist Church tends to change the churches on a circuit with the greatest frequency. Pastors are appointed by the bishop, who determines which congregations shall be on a particular circuit. The best arrangements are those which most benefit the people, not those which serve the clergy's desires or needs.

Compatible Communities and Churches

As much as possible, congregations that are made part of a multi-church parish should be in communities free from undue rivalry. Some competition (often expressed in sporting events) tends to exist among communities located in the same general area. This is a normal aspect of life and produces community spirit and cohesiveness. If it is not taken too seriously, it will not interfere with more serious relationships such as those in business and religious activities. It is sometimes possible to arrange the multi-church parish so that the community factors contribute to cohesiveness. For example, there are parishes in which all the children attend the same public school and the people do a large part of their shopping in the same town. The members of individual churches may thus share an identification with a larger community.

In any case, events in the community can influence relationships among the churches. Community rivalry can jeopardize cooperation between churches. In one area, a bitter battle over school consolidation ended with all the pupils being bussed to the county seat. The residents of one town were angry over the closing of their school, which stood vacant in the center of the community with plywood covering its windows. At this point the denominational officials requested that the congregation become part of a parish with a central office in the county seat. To the people it seemed like another setback for their town. The congregation responded with a firm "No!" The church retained its pastor.

It is particularly important that the churches served by the same pastor have some degree of compatibility. As much as possible, the congregations should be composed of persons who agree about what the church is and what it should be doing, what should be the style of worship and the expected programs. The congregations composing a multi-church parish must share a common theological stance, what it means to be a Christian, and what the nature and mission of the church is. This will make it possible for the members of the different churches to cooperate on parish-wide matters. Furthermore, it will also be advantageous to the pastor as he or she prepares sermons and works to develop programs if those sermons and programs can with only minor modifications be made appropriate for all the churches. To have an effective multi-church parish requires cooperation and compromise by all concerned. If theological compatibility exists, the external factors contributing to divisiveness can be curtailed and those which foster unity can be emphasized.

III.

Where the Minister Lives

The pastor's residence is one of the most important matters the congregations forming a multi-church parish must negotiate. Most congregations own a manse or parsonage or share the ownership of a house occupied by the pastor. Churches that are part of a multi-church parish tend to be located in sparsely populated communities where the options for housing are extremely limited. To obtain a minister, many such churches must provide a residence. A satisfactory arrangement concerning the location and ownership of the pastor's residence and the amount of funds each church pays toward its purchase and maintenance is essential for a smooth running multi-church parish.

Patterns of Home Ownership

There are two patterns of church-owned residences in which multi-church parishes are involved. In the first, one congregation owns the house and the other or others pay a fixed monthly charge. In the second, the churches jointly own the parsonage. Each congregation then pays its share of maintenance costs.

Churches that share a pastor do not appear to have great difficulty coming to a satisfactory agreement over each congregation's share of the minister's housing. When one church owns the house, the other contributes to the cost of maintenance. These amounts are not excessive and are often quite modest, sometimes as low as $50 a month. Some pastors have observed that congregations having a formal written agreement concerning mutual responsibility for long-term maintenance of the parsonage not only avoid misunderstandings and tensions but function more efficiently. Ministers whose churches have such agreements commonly feel that their lives are easier.

When two or more churches jointly own a house, it is necessary for one to purchase the other's equity if the agreement to share the pastor is canceled. The United Methodist Church has a clearly stated policy for such a situation. That denomination requires that when a circuit is divided or realigned, the church or churches which will no longer have their pastor living in the parsonage are to receive their share of equity in the property. The amount owed is based on the current reasonable value of the parsonage. The district superintendent appoints a committee of three persons who are members of churches not on the circuit to determine the value of the parsonage. Such a committee hears all interested parties and takes into account the investment each has made in the parsonage. The church continuing to own the parsonage must purchase the equity of the other church or churches as determined by this committee. If the congregations are not satisfied with the committee's decision, they have the right to appeal to the next session of the annual conference. The decision of the annual conference is final and binding. Any sum of money a congregation receives as its equity in a parsonage may not be applied to current expenses or current budget but must be used for the purchase of or for capital improvements to a parsonage. Some churches do not provide housing for the pastor. In some cases the person called or appointed to a multi-church parish already owns a house. These tend to be lay pastors and others who serve part-time. Many congregations sharing a pastor are in rural areas, and the opportunities for a pastor to obtain suitable housing are limited, yet rural churches may find it necessary to provide housing if they hope to employ an ordained person who will work full-time in the ministry. Occasionally a pastor may wish to be able to purchase a house. This indicates an intention to remain for a long period of time, and such a purchase can add stability and be beneficial if the match between minister and parish is good. However, clergy tenure in multi-church parishes tends to be short. Hence, a church-owned house is virtually a requirement for most multi-church parishes.

The Importance of Where the Minister Lives

The locale of one's residence identifies one with a particular community. Assumptions tend to be made about people based on where they live. This is as true for a minister as it is for a layperson. Certain characteristics are automatically assigned to persons who reside in communities awarded high prestige. In contrast, the individual who comes from a section of town referred to as the "other side of the tracks" is also assumed to have certain social characteristics, generally negative ones. Such stereotyping is of course unfair and unreliable as a means of determining a person's character, but it is practiced nonetheless.

Many local churches are identified with a particular community and the kind of people who are perceived to live there. This may be a rural area, an urban neighborhood, a small town, or a section of a metropolis. The members may perceive themselves as being residents of such places as Centerville or Ingleside Heights. There may be a sense of community, loyalty, and pride that is expressed through participation in institutions identified with the community, such as clubs, athletic teams, volunteer fire companies, schools, and churches. It is therefore not surprising that the

39

members of a particular congregation prefer their pastor to be identified with their church and community. One way this can be accomplished is for the minister to reside in the community the church is located in and where the members live. In most instances where a minister serves only one congregation, the parsonage is located in the same general area as the church. However, when a pastor serves two or more churches, he or she can live in only one community.

The desire for the pastor to be identified not only with the church but also with the community is a strong motivation for congregations not to share their minister with another church. If a pastor can live in the same community as the church and its members, there is no obstacle to becoming identified with that community. The importance of a pastor's being identified with the community of the members of a congregation can be illustrated with an incident in one church located in a small town. The members were reminiscing about a former pastor, an individual who had been much appreciated and who also very closely identified with the life of the village in which the church was located. One laywoman commented, "Reverend Evans was involved in everything in this town. Why, the fire engine never answered a call without his being on it."

The minister of a multi-church parish must make a special effort to identify with the people and communities in which his or her churches are located. This will depend greatly on the quality of relationships the pastor is able to build with other persons in each community. And this takes time: As one minister said, "Five years are a minimum."

The Location of the Minister's Residence

The pastor must live somewhere. Sometimes the residence is in neutral territory. The location should, of course, enable the pastor to be accessible to his or her members. By not being in any of the communities where the churches are located, the minister is not identified with one church to the detriment of the others. Finding a satisfactory neutral community is not always possible, given the location of churches and the distribution of the population. It is not uncommon, particularly in the South, for the parsonage of a multi-church parish to be in the county seat town. This is a location often preferred by the minister's family. The pastor can readily drive out into the rural areas where the churches and members are located, and the people who come to the county seat for business and other reasons can see their pastor should they desire to do so. This has been a much more desirable arrangement than simply putting the residence in an isolated rural setting where there are few other persons in the immediate vicinity.

Some of the most difficult situations have arisen when a minister's residence is located in the vicinity of just one of his or her churches. The problem is that the minister comes to be identified primarily with that church and its community, which leads to the members of the other church becoming dissatisfied. In one two-church parish, the congregations agreed to construct a new residence on available land next to the church in a village. The other church was in a crossroads community about six miles away. An excellent dwelling was constructed, but the outlying congregation was never satisfied with the pastor living next to the one church. The members of the other church in the parish always felt that they were neglected, that the pastor did not give them the appropriate amount of service. The dissatisfaction persisted until the parish was dissolved and a second house built adjacent to the other church. Each congregation now has a part-time pastor and both are happy with the arrangement, each feeling it is receiving adequate pastoral services although it shares its minister with a secular job.

Frequently, multi-church parishes are established with churches that already own houses. The congregations do not have the option of deciding precisely where to erect a

41

parsonage. Generally, the choice is to house the pastor in one of the existing houses and sell or rent the other. Some of the most difficult problems concerning the minister's residence tend to arise when a parish is formed and the congregations must decide which of the dwellings will *not* be used. Although one may be rented and thus produce some income, such an arrangement may not be perceived as satisfactory. Most laypersons would prefer to have the rented house occupied by a minister. After all, they erected the dwelling for their pastor, and the fact that it is not being used tends to injure their pride. It reminds them that they are not financially able to support a full-time minister. They say to themselves, the congregation did not contribute funds to provide housing for our minister simply to have it become rental property.

A variation on having a surplus residence occurs when a clergy couple serves adjacent congregations or even adjacent multi-church parishes. When each congregation or parish owns a parsonage, one will not be needed. Where the ministers will live is a matter that must be worked out between the clergy and the congregations. The issue is complex because the next pastors probably will not be married to each other. A satisfactory arrangement will require sensitivity and compromise by both the pastors and the people.

Nevertheless, the minister serving more than one church can only reside in one community. The churches involved must make compromises if they are to receive the services of a pastor. Several things can be done to help make the situation workable.

Relating to Several Communities

The minister who serves a multi-church parish needs to be aware that the congregations wish him or her to be strongly identified with them and their community. When the pastor does not live in the area it is important to take appropriate steps to help the members feel that this identification does in fact exist. There are two ways this can be done.

First, the minister needs to spend some time each week on a regular basis in the community where he or she does *not* live. The congregation needs to be aware that their pastor does this. Many small churches on circuits do not have an office, so it may be appropriate for the minister to announce that he or she will spend a specific time, such as Tuesday and Friday afternoons from one to three, at that particular church. The pastor needs to be there so that anyone who wishes to see him or her can do so. Even if no one comes, the pastor still has several hours of uninterrupted time for study and sermon preparation. The fact that the minister's car is parked in front of the church is a visible sign to all that the minister is in the community regularly.

One clergy couple serve two churches located in small towns several miles apart. In addition to holding regular office hours in both churches, they make it a practice to eat lunch several times each week in a restaurant in the town where the manse is not located. They are convinced that this gives them visibility which helps offset their living elsewhere.

Second, the pastor needs to be alert to community functions in the various locales where the churches on the circuit are located. Communities may develop traditions and have certain civic events. It is important that the pastor know about these and participate in them if a continuing sense of identification with the various congregations is to be effectively maintained. In many rural areas such events may be infrequent and will not take up a great deal of time. However, the dividends such participation provides will certainly more than offset the investment of the minister's time and effort. One pastor made it a practice to attend the softball games in the community in which one of his three

43

churches was located. He commented, "I can see most of my members at the game and they can see me."

An issue related to the location of the minister's place of residence that arises from time to time is the church participation of the parsonage family. The pastor's spouse and children, of course, can have their membership in only one church. Those churches in communities different from that of the parsonage may feel cheated because the spouse does not share in certain congregational activities. This can become a source of tension where a tradition of participation by the minister's wife has grown up. She may be perceived as living "there," where she takes part in the church, but of ignoring us "over here."

There is of course no simple way of dealing with this issue. We are in a period when role expectations are in flux, and so general rules will not apply in every situation. There are however certain factors to consider. First, the pastor, and to some degree his or her spouse, are public figures. This "comes with the territory" and cannot be avoided. Second, the spouse will to some degree have an impact on the minister's effectiveness. What the spouse does or does not do in a particular situation will depend on the individual's personality, skills, and most important his or her understanding of and commitment to the church.

There is generally no solution concerning where the pastor of a multi-church parish will live that is completely satisfactory to all concerned. Like many aspects of such a parish, sensitivity is required on the part of the pastor and compromise on the part of each of the churches, which must give a little for the good of all. The pastor needs to be alert to differences between the communities in which the churches are located, particularly rivalries that can affect the church. It is essential that the minister make an effort to become identified with the different communities in which the lay members live despite the fact that he or she resides elsewhere.

44

IV.

Managing the Multi-Church Parish Effectively

Managing a multi-church parish is a difficult and complex task. The situation may not be so bad as that described by the pastor who said, "Most clergy would rather not go to multi-church parishes. The word has gotten out that they are a lot of work, probably twice as much work as a larger single church." Nevertheless, the pastor who must manage two or more congregations, each of which is both similar and different, has a demanding job. The churches composing the parish share the denominational tradition, but each also has its own history, style, and personality. The congregations will have some activities in common but also may have their unique programs. Each church will have its own internal organization, which requires the pastor's attention.

The Worship Schedule

The Sunday morning worship service is the major event in the local church. It is the one activity that takes place in every church. No matter how small a congregation may be, it will have regular worship services. It can be argued that the central role of the Christian community is to gather together to worship and to hear the word of God preached.

The tradition of having worship at eleven o'clock on Sunday morning is deeply embedded in American churches. Whatever the reason for this practice, it is the hour at which most Protestant people prefer to worship. Some large congregations now have two services and are finding that an increasing number of people prefer to attend at an earlier hour, but the largest attendance still tends to be at the eleven o'clock hour.

A matter that must be negotiated by congregations which are part of a multi-church parish is the Sunday morning worship schedule. This is often the most difficult matter to resolve. A variety of patterns can be noted. When the parish consists of two churches, each usually has a service every Sunday morning. Sometimes one church will have the eleven o'clock hour for six months and the other an earlier service. The schedule will then be reversed for the next six months. Some pastors say that changes made too frequently in the time of the worship service make it difficult to attract new members. People are not sure when to attend. If the congregations insist on changing, the same schedule of services should be maintained for an entire year.

When a parish consists of four churches, the pattern is for two of the congregations to have worship services on the first and third Sundays and the other two churches to have services on the second and fourth Sundays. In those months when there is a fifth Sunday, the most common practice is not to have a service. Occasionally, a special event such as a music program or an outside speaker involving all of the churches will be held on the fifth Sunday.

When an odd number of churches is involved, working out the worship schedule can be particularly difficult. A variety of practices exist, such as a service every week in the larger church and on alternate Sundays in the two smaller ones. This practice is common where one of the churches has a membership much larger than the other two. In a few cases where distance permits, services are held weekly in all three churches. In an attempt to be fair to all, three church parishes often have very complex worship schedules such as services at one time on the first and third Sundays and at a different time on the second and fourth Sundays.

The Sunday morning worship schedule is the one aspect of the circuit that will probably never be worked out to everyone's complete satisfaction. In determining when the services are held, several factors are usually considered. One is the proximity of the churches and the time needed for the pastor to travel from one to another. Another is the portion of the budget the different churches will provide. If one congregation provides a major share of the finances it may insist on having services every Sunday at eleven. Whatever the arrangements, some degree of accommodation and compromise is necessary if each church is to have as many worship services as possible.

The schedule of worship services is a matter the pastor and the congregations must work out. It requires some degree of compromise by all after a frank discussion of the issues. The schedule must be realistic for the pastor while providing the maximum of opportunities for worship by the people.

The Church School

The inability of the pastor to be present during the church school hour is considered one of the major disadvantages of the circuit. When a congregation wishes to withdraw from a parish, having the pastor participate in the Sunday school is frequently given as a reason for the change. However, having to be present at more than one church on Sunday does not prevent the pastor from giving leadership to the educational program.

It should first be recognized that the Sunday school has often been the most important program in the church that shares a pastor. Worship services may be held only twice a month but Sunday school is in session every week. The pastor may reside in a community some distance away, but the Sunday school superintendent and the teachers live in the local community. In those churches where the minister's tenure tends to be short, the Sunday school provides continuity. The Sunday school superintendent may be the most important leader in the congregation. One pastor commented, "The Sunday school superintendent at Mt. Bethel is a kind of second pastor for the congregation."

Although the minister cannot be present during the church school hour, he or she can still provide important leadership for the educational program. The first and most significant thing the minister can do is to show an interest in the Sunday school. It is important for those persons who teach week after week to know they have the interest and support of their pastor. Just to inquire how the classes are going and show an interest can be important to the teacher.

The minister can give leadership to the educational program by participating in the committee which supervises the Sunday school and other educational programs. The pastor can also take an active part in recruiting church school teachers and arranging opportunities for teacher training. One pastor invited the Sunday school teachers in all of his churches together for a potluck dinner every quarter, at which time they discussed matters relating to their teaching. He or she will know and have access to the denominational staff persons and can arrange for workshops and other events for teachers and leaders.

Finally, the minister should from time to time teach. A special course can be offered occasionally, perhaps in one of the churches or on a parish-wide basis. This would have several benefits. First, it would be good for the members to engage in serious study under the direction of the pastor. Second, it would demonstrate to the people the importance of learning as a means of growing in the faith. Third, preparing to teach a course is an excellent way to gain an understanding of a subject in depth and is therefore an excellent method of continuing education for the minister. Some multi-church parishes with two congregations have an early service at one and a later service at the other, with the Sunday school between the services. This allows the pastor to teach in one church for six months and in the other for the next six months.

Parish-Wide Programs

There is a kind of mystique about cooperative programs which is not justified by their effectiveness or the results they yield. The assumption is that cooperative activities are by definition better than what a congregation may do by itself. Cooperative programs, however, tend to undercut the weaker church. They also tend to be incompatible with growth because the energy goes into cooperation rather than outreach.

There are some opportunities for parish-wide events which can be beneficial to the congregations. It must be clearly recognized that a multi-church parish is made up of two or more individual congregations each with its unique tradition, personality, and needs. Program activities, even if they are parish wide, take place in the individual churches.

Any parish-wide activity must be perceived by the people as something valuable to them as individuals, to their local church, or to some group within their congregation. It must also be something the individual church cannot adequately do by itself. It may be an activity considered essential or one that enriches the life of the church. Furthermore, to have successful joint programs the churches must be located close enough together so that the members can participate without travel being too great a burden.

Some multi-church parishes have had successful joint youth groups. In these cases, each of the congregations had some teenagers but none had a sufficient number to sustain an organized group. Combined youth groups tend to be easier to organize when the youth in the participating churches attend the same high school. It is important that the congregations support the joint youth program and that counselors come from more than one of the participating churches. This is easier to accomplish if the churches are relatively close together and if the members are part of the same larger community.

A variety of short-term enrichment activities are often conducted on a parish-wide basis. One such program is special services with an outside speaker. Musical programs such as congregational hymn singing are popular events in some communities. And training events for church school teachers and other local church officials are conducted for all the churches in a parish.

In arranging for parish-wide programs, the pastor occupies a key role. The pastor is the one person who has continuing contact with all the local churches. He or she is in the best position to know the needs of each of the congregations and their strengths and weaknesses and what outside resources are most appropriate at any given time. The pastor can best judge what joint programs might be most effective.

Cooperative programs are not easy to set up. They involve obtaining the cooperation of different congregations among whom there may be some degree of rivalry. It may mean bringing together people who have not known one another. A parish-wide program tends to require more work by the pastor and take more time than a similar activity in one local church. However, cooperative activities enable some churches of small membership to enrich their ministries in ways that make the extra time and effort worthwhile.

Parish Administration

Effective administration of the circuit is more complex than is generally assumed, even by many pastors. It is complex

50

because the pastor must manage two or more institutions at the same time. Because some of the churches may be small, the administration tends to be quite informal. There often is no central office or minister's study apart from that located in the parsonage. Appropriate office equipment may be minimal or nonexistent. Many such churches are unable to provide any secretarial assistance to the pastor.

Given this situation, the responsibility for the administration of the multi-church parish falls heavily on the pastor. This requires first an understanding of the formal and informal leadership patterns in each of the churches. Small membership churches tend to have decision-making patterns that center on family and informal relationships. Major decisions may be made by the members as they stand around between Sunday school and the worship service. Sometimes they are made apart from the church so that the board meeting becomes a time when the decision is reported rather than made.

The pastor must learn how decisions are made in the different congregations and balance these against the formal requirements of the denomination. This can be difficult because of the limited amount of time a pastor can spend with any one church and in any one community. It is particularly difficult when one of the churches is a long distance from the parsonage, thus limiting informal contacts with church members.

To administer a multi-church parish requires substantial self-discipline and considerable skill on the part of the pastor. Attention must be given to each of the churches on the charge. The minister must continually weigh the conflicting demands on his or her time and decide what can and cannot be done. The pastor must manage to give some time to each of the churches, to learning how each one actually functions, to seeing that the necessary records are maintained, and to seeing that the congregation is organized in a manner appropriate to its size and mission in the community.

Finances

The cost of employing a pastor is for most multi-church parishes the only shared financial responsibility. The financial problems in most multi-church parishes are related to the fact that many of the congregations are small. They may have difficulty raising the amount of money needed for the church program and the support of the pastor. In one case, no particular problems were reported in the churches' being able to come to an agreement on the portion of the cost of employing a minister that each would pay. The exception was when one of the churches decreased or increased in size, making it possible for it to assume a larger share of the costs or requiring it to decrease its contributions. A renegotiation of the agreement was then necessary.

When the parish consists of two congregations of approximately equal strength, the practice is for each to assume 50 percent of the shared costs. This is probably the most common practice and a method that works well. When one of the churches is substantially larger than the other or when the parish consists of three or more churches of different sizes, each congregation's share must be agreed on. In one instance, no particular difficulties were reported in arriving at an equitable division, even though the portions varied widely.

The only point of reported tension over sharing finances in the instance above was when members of the larger church in the parish complained that their congregation was not receiving an appropriate share of the pastor's time. As one person put it, "We are providing three-fourths of Pastor Schwartz's salary but he must be spending at least half of his time at St. John's." Such an attitude does tend to cast ministry into a mechanistic framework and fails to take into account that from time to time needs vary. There will be periods when a congregation requires a majority of the minister's time. There will also be periods when a church will need only minimal attention. One experienced pastor said that she responded to such complaints by saying that all of the churches in the parish had the service of a full-time minister and that she was always available to the persons who needed her.

A pastor serving several churches needs to communicate how his or her time is allocated to the various congregations. When one of the churches needs a large amount of the pastor's time, it is advisable for all the congregations to share in the decision. In one case a pastor was assigned to four churches. One was located in a community into which people were moving. The minister and the three other churches agreed that he would spend a major portion of his time attempting to reach the new residents. The entire parish saw this as their mission responsibility and took great satisfaction in the membership increase that the fourth congregation experienced. There was no feeling that any of the churches were not getting the portion of the minister's time that they were paying for. The pastor was of course careful to see that he was available to the members of all the churches who needed him, but everyone understood that the priority was to win new residents to the church in the growing community.

V.

Advice to the Minister

A prominent denominational official, when asked what three factors contributed most to making a local church effective, replied, "Leadership, leadership, and leadership." Although this response may be a bit oversimplified, it represents the opinion of many persons in the church. No one will argue that leadership is critical in determining the effectiveness of any institution. Just what constitutes good leadership is sometimes hard to define. It is easier to recognize effective leaders than it is to define them with any degree of precision.

The pastor is the most important leader in the local church. It is the minister who stands before the congregation Sunday after Sunday to preach the Word and to lead the people in worship. His or her understanding of the nature and mission of the church will tend to set the tone for the congregation and have considerable influence on what activities the group undertakes. The vision of the minister may become the vision of the people. And though a minister may not be able to persuade all the people to follow his or her leading, it is rare for a congregation to move in a direction the pastor does not wish to go.

The minister's leadership is critical whether he or she is serving a large or small congregation, a single church or a multi-church parish. Different types of churches require different skills on the part of the pastor. The small-membership church may not want a leader in the sense of wanting a person who will move the congregation in a new and different direction. Such a church may want a pastor and preacher, someone who will understand and love them and interpret the gospel on Sunday morning.

The multi-church parish, which usually consists of small churches, has certain characteristics a pastor who wishes to be effective must consider. Let's discuss these characteristics.

Ministry to People

Although the Christian ministry is always carried out in some form of social group, the pastor ministers to individuals. The congregation is made up of people who have desires and ambitions, strengths and weaknesses, joys and sorrows, problems and potential. It is the individual who makes the decision to accept the Christian faith and to become a disciple of Christ. The call to the ministry is a call to minister to individuals. In a society where an increasingly large percentage of the population is concentrated in large urban centers and where the individual may be lost in the mass of people, the Christian church continues to be a place where the individual is of primary concern. Even large urban congregations emphasize helping the individual become part of a smaller group within the congregation.

One of the great satisfactions of the ministry is the opportunity the pastor has to assist individuals on their journey of faith and in many other areas of their lives. The particular form of church organization, the size of a particular congregation, whether the church is in the country or in the city, or whether the pastor serves only one congregation or several, does not detract from either the effectiveness or the satisfactions of ministering to individuals. The person who serves a multi-church parish must be convinced that his or

55

her call is to serve people in whatever institutional form they may elect to organize themselves into. It is of course well known that a minister's status is to some degree determined by the type of church he or she serves. The pastor who is called to a large congregation is awarded higher status than one serving a small-membership church. Secular society tends to equate bigness with importance; unfortunately, this attitude is also found in churches. One pastor commented that he felt like a failure. When asked why, he responded, "This is my third appointment since graduating from seminary and I'm still serving a circuit." He *had* been assigned to three rural congregations, but all were strong churches with a total membership of more than 350. The problem was that he was equating success with having only one church, something which is accepted not only by pastors but also by laypersons and denominational officials.

The pastor who sees his or her task as ministering to people will find satisfaction in whatever institutional setting ministry takes place in. Such a person will be able to adapt to the situation whether it is in an urban or rural environment or whether the assignment or call is to one congregation or to a multi-church parish.

The Local Church as the Basic Unit

The local church is the institution in which the pastor has to work. Although a minister may have responsibility for several congregations, each is an entity. The temptation is for the pastor to perceive the parish as a unit when in reality it is two or more separate and distinct institutions. The person serving a multi-church parish is something like the expert checker player who plays several games at once. Such a player moves from one opponent to the next, making a move at each board. The games all have some things in common but each has its unique characteristics.

In relating to the congregations in the multi-church parish, it is crucial that the pastor realize that each is to some degree different. Like individuals, local churches have personalities. A pastor with more than one church may simply like one of the congregations more than another. He or she may feel more comfortable with one group than with the other or find more satisfaction in relationships with the members. The chemistry between the pastor and the congregations will vary. This is not easy to explain, but is a fact, which both the minister and the church members must recognize. One experienced minister commented on how his experience differed from that of his predecessor. One of the churches in the parish had responded well to his predecessor, had shown an increase in both activity and giving. In the two years since he accepted the call, the reverse was true. The other congregation, which had been static, was experiencing a burst of enthusiasm and activity while the first one had become less active, or as he described it, "almost stagnant."

It is important ministers recognize that congregations will respond to their leadership in different ways. To recognize this fact does not mean that a particular response is inevitable and must be accepted. By understanding the situation, a minister can discover ways to relate to what he or she feels is the more difficult congregation. The natural tendency even for clergy is to put one's time and energy into activities that are rewarding and where results are forthcoming. One pastor in the Midwest, when asked what advice he would give to a minister serving a multi-church parish, replied, "Figure out which church is the smallest and has the least resources and make sure that is not left out. Don't play favorites."

It is important the pastor remember that congregations are not static. They change continually and over time may actually change vastly. The membership may grow old so that a large number of the people are retired. Congregations may also grow younger as new families replace those who die or move away. Different lay leaders may bring a new perspective and a different vision of the mission of the congregation. The pastor needs to be alert for the signs of change that are occurring or may occur in the not too distant future. The effective pastor is one who can understand the nature of the changes taking place in the community and the congregation and not only help the members understand those changes but also help the church meet people's current needs. The minister will from time to time have the opportunity to guide the congregation as it ministers in a changing situation.

Determine Today's Needs

Not only are congregations different, but also their needs and opportunities vary over time. Thus, what may be an appropriate program for a church at one point may be quite inappropriate at another. There is the tendency to continue activities which once were effective but have long outlived their usefulness. Every pastor must continually evaluate the churches' programs to determine whether they continue to be valid. The pastor of a multi-church parish has the task of doing this for more than one congregation. As an outsider who has had professional training, the pastor should be in the best position to help the members determine which activities continue to meet the specific needs of the congregation that the church can and should address. The needs and the appropriate responses may be quite different in each local church. One church may contain a large percentage of senior citizens with the concerns of persons in the later years of their lives. Another congregation may have a large number of young families with small children who present the pastor with an entirely different set of opportunities.

When needs are determined, priorities must be set. Setting new priorities may involve discontinuing some activities, a task which may be difficult. Old habits for people and churches are hard to break. The churches that share a minister tend to have limited resources, which forces the people to decide what they can and cannot do. This is a difficult task because the needs in virtually any community are greater than the available resources. Few things a pastor does are more important than helping the congregation focus their energy and resources so that their ministry can be as effective as possible.

Delegate Responsibility

Because pastors of multi-church parishes simply cannot carry the entire responsibility for the management and program of all the churches for which they have responsibility, they must delegate many tasks to the laity. This is not easy for some ministers because it appears to mean that they are relinquishing a portion of their authority. There is also the feeling on the part of some ministers that the lay members— no matter how well intentioned and dedicated they may be—simply cannot carry on the ministry so well as the pastor, who has had the advantage of seminary training. The debate over whether seminary education produces effective pastors for small churches continues and is unlikely to be resolved. Some insist that something short of seminary training produces pastors who can better serve small churches and they cite studies as evidence. Others claim that every church and lay member should have the services of a minister who meets the educational requirements of the denomination.

The feeling that professional education provides superior ministry is only partly correct. The church throughout its long history has been led by persons with varying degrees of preparation. Formal education in any given period only ensures that the individual has received instruction in what the religious leaders think is appropriate for ordained persons at that point in time. It is not, of course, realistic to expect "professional performance" from lay volunteers. But it is both realistic and appropriate to suppose that the witness and ministry such persons carry on can be effective.

Delegating responsibility requires that the pastor first identify persons within the congregations who can provide leadership. They must be persuaded to give their time and talent to the work of the church. They must then be assisted in gaining the necessary skills and knowledge to carry out their tasks. This requires a substantial amount of work by the pastor. It is often more difficult and time-consuming for a minister to recruit, motivate, and train volunteers than it would be simply to perform the task. However, the congregation is well served by such efforts not only because of the work the volunteers do but also because such work provides an opportunity for them to be enriched and grow in their understanding of the faith.

The importance of being able to delegate responsibility was expressed by a pastor who had spent fifteen years serving a multi-church parish. His advice was, "Learn to delegate responsibility; becoming more advisory. Let the laity learn to lead themselves."

The multi-church parish requires that the pastor and people share in the ministry of the churches. Because churches are in different communities often some distance apart, the minister simply cannot be present much of the time. More of the work of the church must be done by laypersons if the churches are to have an effective ministry. Let's next discuss specific tasks of the laity.

VI.

Suggestions for the Laity

Lay members carry a large share of the responsibility for the ministry of a church when the pastor serves one or more congregations located in different communities. The more churches in the parish, the less time and energy the pastor has to devote to each. The distances between the churches mean that they are "on their own" for more or less extended periods of time because the minister is in one of the other communities. The effectiveness of any local church, and particularly of those in a multi-church parish, depends on the way the laity and the clergy work together and support each other.

Lay Responsibility for Ministry

Within the Protestant tradition, the responsibility for the ministry of the church has been shared by the laity and the clergy. Lay members are not expected to passively await orders from the clergy or limit their participation to providing the necessary funds. In fact, the line which divides the tasks of ordained from non-ordained persons is at times somewhat blurred. Although there are variations among denominations, the authority to administer the sacraments of the Lord's Supper and Baptism tends to be restricted to the clergy. Preaching is primarily the responsibility of the clergy, but proclaiming the gospel and witnessing to the faith are by no means limited to those who are ordained. Although the vast majority of worship services are conducted and sermons preached by those who have been duly authorized, laypersons in a variety of ways can teach and interpret the word of God.

The concept of the priesthood of all believers is deeply rooted in Protestantism. Some denominations formally recognize the role of the laity in the total ministry of the church. For example, The United Methodist Church refers to the general ministry of all Christian believers (the laity) and to the representative ministry of those set apart for special tasks (the clergy). All Christians are seen as having been called to minister wherever Christ would have them serve and to witness in deeds and in words. The clergy are perceived as those who have special gifts, are called by God, and are ordained to serve in specific ways.

Lay members of congregations that share a minister simply must assume more responsibility, not only for the operation of the church but also for more aspects of the ministry. Although the pastor should be available to perform the tasks required of an ordained person, the responsibility for several congregations may require greater lay participation. The minister who is responsible for several congregations is simply not available to do all that might be done in each of the churches and their communities. Some of the areas where laypersons must give leadership include the educational program and some types of pastoral care.

In many multi-church parishes, the Sunday school has been the strongest and best attended activity. In those churches which do not have a weekly worship service, the church school usually meets every Sunday. It may be the only regular activity that takes place so frequently. The Sunday school has traditionally been led by laypersons. In some rural churches the superintendent of the Sunday school is the most important leader in the congregation. When the pastor cannot be present during the church school hour, leadership for the educational program must be provided in other ways, such as teacher training. This does leave the lay members with the greater share of responsibility for carrying on the educational ministry of the congregation and total responsibility for what happens on Sunday morning.

The Sunday school has been where Christian people have learned the meaning and nature of their faith. It is where individuals are taught the content of the Bible and the history of the Christian church. In this way they come to understand their tradition and make it a part of their lives. Teachers are role models for children and youth. Joining a Sunday school class is a way for new persons to become integrated into the congregation. And the entire educational program in the small multi-church parish is led by laypersons.

Lay members in multi-church parishes also share in what might be called pastoral care. Small congregations tend to function like extended families and respond almost instinctively to crises and needs of members. Because the people know one another well, they know when a situation requiring assistance arises in one of the member families. They can be supportive and provide a variety of aid in times of crisis. Depending on the particular need, the pastor may or may not be involved.

The pastoral care provided by lay members takes a variety of forms. A group of church members regularly telephone an elderly member to see that she is all right. Others provide child care when a mother is hospitalized. In one instance the pastor became pregnant. During her maternity leave the congregation not only assisted the minister and her family but also assumed many of the pastoral care responsibilities normally left to the clergy.

It is important that laypersons understand the importance of their contribution to the ministry of the church. The trend in most denominations has been for the clergy to become increasingly professional. Four years of college and three years of theological seminary education are more and more the accepted norm for entrance into the ministry. This has in some instances made the laity reluctant to engage in certain types of ministry because they do not have the training required of the ordained clergy and thus feel inadequate. The members of congregations that share a pastor must assume responsibility for some aspects of the ministry of their church. If they fail to take initiative in witnessing to the faith, caring for one another, and serving the larger community these tasks will not be done.

What to Expect of the Pastor

Congregations have a right to expect certain things from their pastor whether they are or are not part of a multi-church parish. Foremost of these is worship services. Worship and preaching are at the center of the life of the church and these are the primary responsibility of the minister. The schedule will vary with the number of churches in the parish and the distance between each, but the laity correctly expect that regularly scheduled worship services will be held in each church. It is also expected that the services will be well led and will include a well-prepared, thoughtful, and relevant sermon.

The members should expect their pastor to be available to them in times of special need and to perform the rituals. These will include such events as the death and funeral of a member. Also included will be baptisms, membership training, confirmation, and wedding ceremonies. Such functions are the responsibility of clergy, who must be ready to serve members' needs as they arise.

The laity who are members of multi-church parishes do in fact have the services of a full-time minister. Their pastor is devoting full time to the work of the churches and is therefore a full-time minister. Other than the multiple worship services and administration of several separate churches, the situation is not very different from that of a large church in respect to pastoral services to individuals. Although the pastor may not live in the community, he or she is available to persons when needed.

The members of churches sharing a pastor cannot expect him or her to be present at every community, congregational, or Sunday school function. There are many local events in which a resident minister would normally participate, but the person with responsibility for more than one church will simply not have time to be present at some of these. Participation will be particularly limited if there is considerable distance between the communities in which the churches are located.

It is important that the pastor have clear priorities on the use of time and that these be communicated to the lay members. Members need to know the basis for their minister's decisions on the use of time. The people will then understand what their pastor perceives to be important and why he or she has elected to be in one place rather than another. The lay members cannot expect the pastor of a multi-church parish to take part in every function, but they can expect to know the criteria used to decide which functions are attended. It is often better if the leaders of the congregation help determine the criteria by which the minister allocates his or her time. In so doing, the people and the pastor would come to have more or less the same priorities.

Keep the Pastor Informed

Communications in churches of small membership and in rural communities tends to be informal. Information is shared by one person telling another, who tells another, and so on. Because the number of persons involved tends to be

65

small, it is frequently possible for a large portion of the congregation to come into contact with one another during the course of a week. One pastor who lived in a village said he saw a large portion of his members by going at a certain time to pick up his mail at the post office every day. Another accomplished the same end by having breakfast in the local cafe. This contrasts sharply with a large church in an urban area where a relatively small number of the members see one another in settings other than the church building and at times other than Sunday morning. In large congregations the weekly newsletter is essential to keep members informed; in small congregations it may be quite unnecessary.

Because the parsonage is in a community different from that of some of the congregations, the minister may at times miss information communicated by the local informal system. It is therefore very important that someone inform the pastor when there is a situation in one of the churches that requires attention. The complaint of some pastors serving multi-church parishes is that persons living some distance from the parsonage fail to pass along vital information about needs or plans the congregation has. In one instance the pastor of four churches arrived to conduct services one Sunday to discover that the church had been painted inside and out and that new carpet had been installed. Though pleased at the initiative of the congregation, he observed that "It would have been nice to have at least known what was planned." A more serious incident occurred when a minister arrived at a church some distance from the parsonage only to discover that one of the members had died unexpectedly the preceding Tuesday. A pastor from another denomination had conducted the funeral service two days later. It is important that the members of multi-church parishes assume responsibility for keeping their pastor informed. It is also important that the pastor take the initiative to build a communications network that will ensure that appropriate information reaches him or her.

When a minister lives some distance from the churches, a call to the parsonage may mean paying long distance charges. Members may be a bit reluctant to phone the pastor if the call is long distance, even when it is important for them to do so. Some congregations have solved this problem by putting an item in the church budget for such calls. The members are instructed that they may phone the minister and reverse the charges. No person therefore needs to feel reluctant to make a collect call to the pastor. Those churches having adopted such a practice have discovered that the costs have not been excessive. Most persons do not reverse the charges, but the fact that they are able to do so eliminates any hesitation to phone the minister.

What the Laity Can Do

Ministry requires the joint effort of the laity and the clergy. The members of the clergy have been called, trained, and ordained to perform certain tasks. There are, however, certain tasks that only the lay members of a local church can do. These are as necessary as the tasks of the clergy. Lay members may not think about these tasks but simply perform them. Although such functions are carried on in all types and sizes of congregations, they are particularly significant for the small congregation that is part of a multi-church parish.

The most important thing the laity do is to decide the ethos of the congregation. By this is meant those multiple factors which determine how the people live out their faith. It includes what they believe, how they feel about their church, and how they communicate these beliefs and feelings to one another and to the community. The ethos of the congregation is hard to define with any precision. It is an attitude that communicates what kind of people make up the congregation. It lets visitors know whether they are welcome and will feel comfortable in this church. In a variety of subtle ways, it tells if this church is really open to receiving newcomers into its fellowship or whether it is an exclusive group.

Most congregations consider themselves friendly and open to all who might attend. After all, the members know one another well and feel very much at home in the group. Because the members of the small church share in the fellowship, they may be unaware that others are excluded. It is necessary for the members to stand back and look at themselves with as much objectivity as possible and ask such questions as, How do those outside the congregation perceive us? Is their perception accurate? What kind of congregation are we? and, Are we the kind of church we want to be?

The members of churches that share their pastor must find prospective members and bring them into the church. The evangelistic outreach of these churches must be primarily the responsibility of the laity. It is difficult, if not impossible, for a non-resident minister to find the persons who are potential members. In fact, one serious, if not the most serious, handicap of the multi-church parish is the difficulty the pastor has in locating, cultivating, and winning new members.

It is essentially the lay members who can bring new persons into the fellowship of the congregation. The non-resident pastor's contribution to the integration of new members is limited. In the case of a large congregation with several hundred members, the individual joins the church and then finds a place in one or more groups such as a Sunday school class, the women's, men's, or youth organizations, the choir, or an interest group. Because there are a variety of organizations which have different purposes and are made up of persons of different ages and interests, the individual can find a place to fit in, make friends, and become part of the fellowship. The larger the church, the smaller the percent of members the individual can know well. In contrast, when someone joins a small church, he or she immediately becomes a part of the entire congregation. There are not the variety of sub-groups in which the individual can find a place. Thus, all the lay members are responsible for making everyone a vital part of the local church.

Ultimately, the effectiveness of any local church depends on the ability of the pastor and the laity to work together to witness and minister in the community for which they have responsibility. Those persons who are members of churches that share a minister have the added task of carrying on the work of the congregation when the pastor cannot be present. Christians have always believed—and the history of the church has continually verified—that God has been able to use the talents of any man or woman who has sought to live a life of faithful service. The multi-church parish today provides the opportunity for the laity to witness to their faith and to minister in the name of Christ. What they do is not only significant but also vital for the work of the church in our time.

VII.

The Cooperative Parish

Four pastors in a rural area in the Northeast were meeting with a representative of a denominational agency. "Between us, we have ten churches," said George, a young pastor two years out of seminary, "and the distance between the two farthest apart is barely over thirty miles." Ed, who was beginning his fifth year as pastor of three churches, continued, "This seems to be a perfect place for a cooperative parish. This area is not going to experience an increase in population. Some of the communities actually have fewer residents than they did twenty years ago. We could cut overhead and have a more effective ministry if we worked together." Dr. Snyder had been listening intently. "You are right on track," he said. "I'm sure the mission society will provide some funds for three years on a decreasing annual basis to help you get started. By that time the cooperative parish should be strong enough to continue without subsidy."

For approximately half a century, the idea of grouping a number of congregations, usually from six to twelve, into a parish served by a staff of clergy and lay professionals as a way to provide a more effective ministry has been an article of faith for many church leaders. This form of organization includes several versions, but it tends to require a high level of cooperation by both the clergy and lay members of the various churches. Our focus does not permit a detailed account of all the issues, problems, and solutions surrounding cooperative parishes. However, it is important and germane to look at the nature and functioning of what can be termed cooperative parishes. Some form of cooperative parish continues to be advocated by many clergy and denominational leaders as the best way to provide adequate pastoral services and programs for small congregations, particularly small churches in rural communities. The cooperative parish has been talked about, written about, and promoted as the way to organize small churches. Some have had periods of success in certain localities. In the main, however, they have not lived up to the expectations of their proponents. In the light of the less-than-outstanding performance of most cooperative parishes, the question can be raised why there is continuing enthusiasm for this particular type of structure.

First, we must look at what is generally understood to be a cooperative parish. Although they may take somewhat different forms, cooperative parishes have several characteristics in common. First, they consist of several churches, which at one time were either served by one pastor or shared a minister with another church. The number of congregations in a cooperative parish is too large to be served by one pastor. The individual churches or multi-church parishes which become part of a cooperative parish were each served before by a different minister. Becoming part of a cooperative parish assumes that each participating congregation will give up some autonomy for the common good.

Second, the churches which tend to be grouped together into a cooperative parish are those located in rural communities. Although cooperative parishes are found in urban areas and among stable populations too, many are located in communities that are not likely to increase in population or are decreasing. Churches declining in membership may have difficulty raising sufficient funds to employ a pastor. This causes members to fear that their church will not survive. The cooperative parish for some may be seen as a possible way of obtaining a pastor, getting a broader program, and doing so with less money, thus helping to ensure the churches' future. In other cases the pastors serving the churches see the cooperative parish as a way of increasing the variety and effectiveness of their church's ministry which was the original intent of the programs when they were first designed.

Third, cooperative parishes often tend to consist of churches that, because of their location, have difficulty obtaining ministerial leadership. Some are in sparsely populated, isolated communities where part-time clergy who also hold secular positions may not be available. The seminary-trained pastor with seven years of education may resist moving to a small out-of-the-way community or be unhappy with the limitations inherent in three of four small congregations. The appeal to a prospective pastor is that he or she will be part of a group of clergy in which the individuals can use their special skills. The cooperative parish is a way for small churches to have the services of a staff, each member of which has certain abilities.

Fourth, cooperative parishes may receive a denominational subsidy, at least in the early years of the parish's life. So great has been the faith of American Protestant Church leaders in cooperative parishes, that it is fairly common for churches to receive financial aid from the judicatory or a national church agency to encourage the formation of a cooperative parish. This aid may be used to supplement ministerial and other staff salaries, provide for an office and equipment, and support certain programs. Such subsidy is often provided as an incentive to get the parish organized, with the hope that the membership will increase and the value of the parish will be sufficiently obvious and the results so beneficial to the congregations that the members will be able and willing to meet the extra costs of its operation. Unfortunately, the subsidy may only be used to support the expectations of higher clergy salary. The outside funds are used to meet the higher costs of operating the cooperative parish, not directly to make the ministry more productive.

Fifth, the congregations that make up a parish tend to be affiliated with the same denomination. Although there are cases where churches of different denominations are working together, these are relatively rare. These usually are in places where a small church of a particular denomination is isolated and, to have a minister at all, it must obtain the services of a pastor who is also serving churches of another communion. Cooperation across denominational lines more often tends to be in community projects in which all have a mutual interest other than participation in a formal organization. The differences in polity and the competition among denominations tend to work against multi-denominational cooperative parishes.

How Cooperative Parishes Get Started

Cooperative parishes may first be formed through the efforts of the denominational leaders. Officials responsible for clergy placement often find small, rural churches difficult to fill. Most clergy do not seek out such churches. The salaries are relatively low; the opportunities for growth may be limited or nonexistent. The possibility of creative church programs seems remote; the sense of isolation may be great. The cooperative parish is perceived as a way of overcoming some of these handicaps. The prospective pastor is assured the circuit will not be isolated but will be part of a team ministry. There will be a close working relationship with colleagues who, it is hoped, will bring special skills to the situation. The individual then is not simply to be the pastor of small churches, but part of an exciting, continuing, larger parish with a varied program.

Judicatory officials want to provide the best possible pastoral leadership to small churches. They tend to be reluctant to send the untrained part-time pastor to a church, knowing that this individual can provide only limited service because of lack of training and full-time secular employment. By combining a number of congregations into a parish, officials can obtain denominational subsidy to support a staff of several ordained clergy to provide ministerial services to a group of churches.

A second source of cooperative parishes is the clergy themselves. It may be that several ministers who are congenial and who work well together find themselves serving churches in the same geographic area. Because of the limited resources in any one particular congregation and because of their association and friendship, the ministers may develop interchurch activities. These might include a county-wide youth program, joint evangelistic services, or a great day of singing. Such joint activities can evolve into a formal organization with a parish-wide committee, a central office, a shared secretary, a parish budget, and a newsletter. Often, denominational subsidy will be sought to help maintain the extra expenses, at least in the initial phase.

Why the Continued Faith in Cooperative Parishes

In the several decades of their existence, in the author's opinion, there is no conclusive evidence that cooperative parishes necessarily produce stronger local churches. Declining churches have tended to continue to decline and stable churches have remained stable before, during, and after their participation in a cooperative parish. The cooperative parish does not seem to be a factor that significantly influences the institutional well-being of congregations. This is the case in spite of the fact that one of the arguments often made for establishing and subsidizing cooperative parishes is that they will grow into strong,

74

self-supporting organizations. In fact in this circumstance, cooperation and growth tend to be incompatible goals in terms of the time and energy of the congregation. Evangelistic outreach must be done with time and energy beyond that required to maintain the parish.

The question may legitimately be asked why there has been such a fascination with cooperative parishes and why they have remained so popular over so long a time, in light of their performance. One of the reasons I believe is the term *cooperative*. In an era of emphasis on ecumenism the word *cooperation* has appeal. Although it may not be said explicitly, competition (which does exist between churches and between denominations) is perceived to be bad.

A more important reason is the model of the local church on which the cooperative parish is built. The model is the large urban church. Although there are many small city-congregations, the model for the cooperative parish is one with enough members to employ, in addition to a senior minister, a director of Christian education, a secretary, possibly an assistant pastor, and other full-time or part-time music and custodial staff as necessary. It is also a church with a sufficiently large pool of members to be able to staff the various offices the denomination expects.

The cooperative parish is an attempt to make possible for smaller churches the organization and program that is possible in large churches. Pastors are instructed by denominational agencies on the kinds of activities that should be the norm in their churches. The pastors of the small membership churches want to do a good job and follow the guidance of their denomination, but the limited membership and resources of their churches tend to make this very difficult. The cooperative parish can, at least theoretically, provide a sufficient membership base to have what is sometimes referred to as "a full church program." Furthermore, the cooperative parish, in theory, permits the specialization that can be found among the staff members of the large congregation. One minister can attend to education, another to evangelism, another to pastoral counseling, and so on. Each pastor can have the opportunity to exercise a professional specialty or pursue a particular interest. The parish collectively is viewed by the clergy as a large congregation; the only difference is that it does not gather for worship and education at the same time in the same building.

There are, of course, certain advantages to the cooperative parish. In addition to a fuller program of ministry, it can have a positive influence on clergy morale. The individual pastors do not feel the sense of isolation and loneliness that they might otherwise feel. This is probably one of the cooperative parish's more significant contributions though not its principal justification for being. There may be a central office, a secretary, regular staff meetings, and high quality office equipment. There is the self-discipline required when one is responsible to colleagues. The group provides both mutual support and a sense of fellowship. At the same time it must be recognized that the cooperative parish is attempting to build an institution around the professional expectations of the clergy and the organization defined as normative by the denomination. However, the world in which the clergy are called to witness and to serve is a world built around people and relationships; whatever structure and institutions are developed should support this calling.

The cooperative parish may also bring in outside resources, which might or might not be available to the individual congregations or multi-church parishes. A prominent speaker may be engaged for an evangelistic campaign. A musical program may be sponsored by the several churches. Special training programs may attract enough persons to justify the expense of bringing an expert from the judicatory staff or even from a national agency.

Finally, there is the outside financial support. The cooperative parish sometimes makes it possible for many such churches and their pastors to obtain aid from their regional judicatory or mission society. Such aid is less likely to be available to individual congregations.

The Life Cycle of Cooperative Parishes

Cooperative parishes, like all finite institutions, tend not to continue indefinitely. Certain circumstances contribute to their dissolution. The cooperative parish founded by either denominational officials or the pastors on the scene tends to exist as long as these persons remain in office and are interested in its continuing. In those parishes started by the clergy themselves, the tendency is to continue as long as none of the pastors relocates. However, ministers at some point will move to another church. Although the length of time a pastor remains will vary among different denominations, the tendency is for the individual to stay a shorter period in a small rural church than in a larger urban congregation. The new minister or ministers will not be a member of the friendship group out of which the parish developed. The newer pastor on the scene may feel very much an outsider. The cooperative parish may contribute to a sense of the newcomer's isolation. The newcomer may prefer to work alone or to concentrate on a different area of ministry from his or her predecessor's specialty.

Cooperative parishes founded by the pastors which survive one or two changes of personnel are rare. The parish may continue for a while, particularly if it is receiving financial support from the judicatory. Nevertheless, the programs and mutual activities will tend to suffer. In time, the component churches usually revert to the status they had before the cooperative parish was formed.

If the motivating factor behind the parish was a judicatory official, it is possible that the next person to occupy that office will have different priorities. This person may not have an interest in the parish and let it wither. When someone for whom the cooperative parish is not a priority assumes the judicatory position, the parish's decline or discontinuance is ensured.

Authority

A continuing problem of cooperative parishes is the matter of authority. The question always is: Who is in charge? By its very nature the parish assumes the willing cooperation of both laity and clergy. However, disagreements and conflicts do arise. Some persons may not always cooperate the way they are expected to do. Disagreements may occur among the clergy. Adjudicating such matters within the cooperative parish is an issue that must be seriously addressed.

Most parishes have someone designated as director. This is usually one of the pastors, perhaps one of the more mature and experienced persons. This person may be called director or coordinator and possibly be paid a somewhat higher salary, the extra amount frequently provided by the denomination for the additional work and responsibility.

Just what authority and power such a coordinator or director really has, however, is often unclear. Is this person expected to persuade the parties to cooperate and do what they should do? Does the director have authority to order the recalcitrant clergy to follow a certain course of action? The parish director may or may not have any authority over the persons assumed to be on the staff. The director may have no voice, or minimal voice, concerning who will become pastors of the participating churches and thus members of the cooperative parish staff. The only authority a director may have is the degree to which the support of the other persons making up the staff can be won. The issue of authority, accountability, and problem resolution must be clearly understood and defined in a cooperative parish.

The situation is quite different from that of the large urban church where the senior pastor is clearly the one in charge. A senior minister will have a voice in determining who will be called or appointed as associate and assistant pastors.

Indeed, he may be the one who decides who shall be employed. He will certainly be a key person in determining which laypersons are employed by the church. This is much less likely to be the case with the director or coordinator of a cooperative parish.

Staff relationships within the cooperative parish tend not to have clear lines of authority and accountability. This causes the organization to be unstable and contributes to the limited life-span of a cooperative parish.

Serious Weaknesses

Although there are advantages to the cooperative parish, particularly for ministers, this form of organization has very serious weaknesses, which make it an unlikely candidate to become a norm in Protestant churches.

The first is the nature of the small membership church. People join a congregation, a specific local church. The reasons for their choice are many and complex. Nevertheless, they pick a specific church because they have experiences there which are significant and meaningful. The loyalty of the laypersons is to Mt. Gilead or Piney Grove or Bethel church. They support their church with their time, talent, and resources because they feel it is worthwhile. In contrast, the clergy may have a model of the church which is not congruent with that of the laypersons. The laity may be happy with their church as it is; the pastor, on the other hand, may see his or her role as working for change. The laypersons may not be explicit in their rejection of what the pastor is trying to do; they may simply refuse to go along, remaining passive so that nothing really changes.

A second weakness is that laypersons want to relate to a specific pastor. They want to know their pastor. In the cooperative parish, whereas the clergy may see themselves as a team, the members are uncertain about staff relationships and how they relate to particular individuals.

Laypersons tend to be uncertain just who their pastor is. A common practice is for services to be held every Sunday in every church. To do this, it is often necessary not only to use the ordained pastors but also to arrange for a series of lay speakers or other persons to conduct services. In one parish with two ministers serving six congregations, services were held in every church every Sunday. A third person was found who could conduct services in two churches while the ministers each held services in other churches. However, this meant that the same person preached in the same church only one Sunday out of three. The parish existed for several years and was perceived by denominational leaders to be very effective. However, one loyal lay member commented, "You don't really know who your pastor is and you *never* know who's going to be there to preach on Sunday." A clear perception of who's in charge and who's a given member's pastor is important to the ministry of a cooperative parish.

A third serious problem with the cooperative parish is that it tends to introduce another layer of organization. Each church is not only expected to carry on its normal activities and committees, but also to have representatives on a parish-wide council. This does not take the place of organization at the local church level but rather creates additional structures. In some cases it siphons off leadership from the congregation or adds to an already overburdened laity. Laity need to be prepared to seriously support the organization of the cooperative parish if it is to be feasible.

On the positive side it must be said that the cooperative parish has in many instances provided a structure by which churches of small membership have witnessed to the gospel and ministered to the communities in which they are located. It is a form that in certain situations can be useful for a period of time. It has not become, and is not likely to become, the normative organization for all small churches. It will not replace the multi-church parish as the method of providing pastors for small churches.

VIII.

The Future of the
Multi-Church Parish

"The people drive into town five days a week to work.
They do their shopping in the mall. I don't see why they
cannot also attend church in town. The three churches on
this circuit can barely provide the required minimum salary
for the pastor. When the annual conference raises this figure
next year I don't think they will be able to come up with the
needed funds." These comments were made by a judicatory
official who had just received a request for funds to subsidize
a pastor's salary.

"I pastor four churches and therefore can preach in each
only twice a month. All of the buildings are old and not really
adequate by today's standards. These congregations ought
to merge and build a new church at some central location. No
one would have to drive more than ten miles to attend and
most of the people would have to come less than six miles."
These comments were made by a minister serving a
multi-church parish consisting of four congregations.

"These churches haven't changed in at least twenty-five
years and I don't see any likely changes in the next
twenty-five years. The members are fine people and they
have been good to me, but I'd like to be in a place where

something was happening." This was the way a young pastor described the two congregations she had been serving in the year-and-a-half since her graduation from seminary.

The above are some typical reactions to the multi-church parish. Although this form of local church organization has long been a prominent part of American Protestantism, it is still looked on with ambivalence. In this final chapter we want to consider some of the trends in both the larger society and in the denominations that are having an impact on the multi-church parish. We will conclude with some suggestions about what might be done to increase the effectiveness of the ministry and witness of these congregations.

A Continuing Issue

The basic fact the Protestant denominations and their clergy must face is that there are—and will continue to be—large numbers of small membership churches without sufficient resources to justify or be able to support a full-time pastor. Many, but not all, of these churches are located in communities in which the population is also small. There simply are not enough current or potential members for these churches to have a full-time pastor and the kind of program perceived to be the denominational norm. Furthermore, some persons prefer the intimacy and informal style of the small church. One pastor serving two congregations not far from a city of more than 35,000 commented, "The people who join my church do so because they prefer a small and informal congregation. Some new families in this community attended for a time but gravitated to one of the larger churches in town. One told me that they preferred the variety of activities that a large church could offer. The people who stayed prefer the kind of church we are." As long as there are people who want to be members of small congregations there will be such churches, and many of them will have to share a pastor.

A temptation for some denominational officials is to try to merge several small churches. The argument goes something like this. "Stoney Creek has 68 members, Pleasant Green has 91, and Thornton Chapel has 87. They could join together and have 246 members. They could have services at eleven o'clock every Sunday. With only one building to heat and maintain, the savings would be substantial."

Although the argument seems logical, the fact is that most congregational mergers are not successful. Despite their record some denominational officials continue to advocate them and manage to cite an example of one somewhere that worked. A good rule of thumb is that after five years the merged congregation will have about as many members as the largest of its component parts. There are several reasons for this phenomenon.

First, local churches are not identical; they are not like branch offices or fast food restaurants. Each congregation has its history, traditions, and leadership. Each has its own culture. A merger means bringing together these different cultural groups. Furthermore, there is strong loyalty to place. A merger will require abandoning the familiar place by all or some of the parties. This means leaving the sacred place where many important events in the members' lives took place. It may mean leaving the place where the individual was baptized, converted, married, and where his mother's funeral was held.

What is more, the size of a congregation determines to a great degree the way it functions. To merge three 80-member congregations to create a church of 240 persons is an attempt to create a different kind of church. The individual who is comfortable in the smaller church may not be comfortable in the larger. Persons who wanted to be members of a larger church would not have remained in a small one and thus may see the increase in size as negative.

There are of course some instances when mergers are appropriate and successful. They are always complex and high risk operations. The instances in which congregational mergers are counterproductive far outnumber those that achieve the desired results. They tend not to make a *large* congregation out of several small ones, but one *small* congregation out of several small ones. Denominational leaders must devise strategies for small congregations and multi-church parishes that are not built on the idea of mergers.

Ministers for Multi-Church Parishes

Although there will continue to be a large number of small churches, the increasing professionalization of the clergy is having an impact on the way these congregations are perceived and the desirability of a call or appointment to a multi-church parish. The expectation now is that persons preparing for the ordained ministry will complete four years of college and three years of theological seminary. Beyond the formal education are the various requirements set by the denomination, which may include an internship and a period of probationary status. Although some denominations have alternative routes to ordination which require less formal education, the expectation is that the candidate for ordination will meet the maximum qualifications. Fewer persons are being admitted into the ministry by the alternative routes. Since it is assumed by the clergy and the denominational leaders that all congregations irrespective of size should be served by a pastor who has completed seminary and been ordained, large numbers of small churches will not meet the expectations of this increasingly professional clergy.

Another trend of the past decade and a half that may increase the number of ordained persons willing to serve small multi-church parishes is a growing number of women entering the ministry. Ordained women clergy do not appear any more willing than men to serve what are perceived to be the less desirable churches, but many are part of two-career families, which may limit their mobility. When both husband and wife are employed, the ordained person may be limited to finding a church in a particular geographic area. The result sometimes is that women ministers may accept a call by or an appointment to a small congregation or a multi-church parish because of its location. Because the non-clergy partner is employed, the minister may be willing to serve such a parish on a part-time basis. The same is true in regard to clergy couples where two full-time churches in proximity are not available. Furthermore, some women clergy with young children prefer a less demanding church in order to have more time to devote to their families. The result is that some ordained clergy are available to serve small churches that might otherwise experience difficulty obtaining a pastor.

There continues to be discussion of "tentmaking" or bi-vocational ministers (that is, clergy who in addition to being pastor of a local church also hold a secular job). The issues related to this are sometimes confused. Actually, there are two distinct groups of bi-vocational pastors and they are quite different.

The first are those persons who have completed the educational requirements and have been ordained. This concept of the ordained person earning his or her living in a secular occupation seems to appeal to denominational executives who have trouble finding pastors for small congregations and multi-church parishes. There is a kind of romantic appeal to the idea of a "tentmaking" minister. However, relatively few clergy elect this option. The fact is that the person who feels called into the ministry and has spent a minimum of seven years preparing for that profession wants to work at it full time. He or she does not want to drive a taxi or work in the supermarket, but to devote as much time and energy as possible to the ministry. Furthermore, the Master of Divinity degree, which prospective clergy earn in theological school, is a professional degree which primarily prepares the individual to be a pastor of a church. It has little marketable value if the holder wishes to enter another line of work either on a full-time or part-time basis. If the churches of small membership are to have the services of an ordained pastor who has received the required training and the minister is to devote full time to his or her calling, multi-church parishes will be with us in large numbers for the indefinite future.

The number of seminary-trained part-time bi-vocational clergy will increase if there are not enough congregations or multi-church parishes to employ them full time. Some persons may be happy with a dual career but there is also the possibility of considerable frustration. Theological education is long and expensive. Furthermore, the expectation of the denominations is for full-time service in the ministry. Although the situation varies among denominations, the idea of a tentmaking pastor is still not the norm.

There is a second category of bi-vocational pastors, who serve a large number of churches. This is a group whose numbers appear to be increasing. They are the men and women whose primary source of income has always been from secular employment but who also serve as pastor of a church or churches on a part-time basis. Many are not graduates of a theological seminary but have taken the special short courses or correspondence courses required by their denomination. Many received their call to the ministry at a time in their lives when it was impossible to complete the education required for ordination. People who serve as bi-vocational pastors can be found in virtually every occupation. A few examples include an elementary school principal, a supermarket manager, a farmer, a mortician, a factory worker, and a rural mail carrier (who delivered mail to a large number of her parishioners).

Bi-vocational ministers are making a significant contribution to the church. They are providing pastoral services to thousands of small congregations unable to employ a full-time ordained person. Many are serving multi-church parishes of two and sometimes more congregations when the total membership is still too small to support a minister full time. It is not an exaggeration to say that large numbers of small churches would simply not be able to continue without the services of a bi-vocational minister.

The part-time bi-vocational pastor brings certain advantages to the small church or multi-church parish. He or she is not simply putting in time in a small church while waiting for a call to a larger situation. Bi-vocational pastors may have had a call to preach, but their career is not only in the church. They do not look to "move up" in the ecclesiastical hierarchy. They are serving small churches because they want to do so, and they tend to bring a sense of enthusiasm to their work.

Many congregations are better satisfied with a bi-vocational pastor than being part of a large multi-church parish. They would rather have their own part-time non-ordained pastor even if he or she is also employed in a secular occupation. The bi-vocational pastor may identify with the church in a way that the person desiring to move on does not. And the fact that such a minister has a job may mean that he or she can stay with the church for a long period of time.

The evidence is that there will be a large number of multi-church parishes for the indefinite future. Some will be served by full-time ordained ministers. There will also continue to be a large number of bi-vocational ministers, some of whom will be ordained and some non-ordained depending on the requirements of their denomination. These persons will serve small congregations and some of the smaller multi-church parishes. Without the multi-church parish and the bi-vocational pastors, many congregations would not have a pastor.

Yesterday's Churches in Today's World

American society tends to value what is new, large, and growing. None of these are characteristics of the congregations composing multi-church parishes. These churches tend to be small, stable, and in some instances declining in membership; many have been in existence for many years. The result is that some clergy and denominational leaders look upon such congregations as not measuring up to what a church ought to be. They may perceive them to be more of a problem than an opportunity for ministry.

Furthermore, the small congregations that are part of a multi-church parish fail to meet the career expectations of many clergy. Ministers, like the laity, have been influenced by the culture in which they live and therefore expect to move ahead in their careers. This means moving from a small church to a large one, from a rural community to an urban area, and from a multi-church parish to a single congregation. Being pastor of two or more rural churches is seen by some as a place to begin but also a place from which to move as soon as possible. As one minister put it, "I look at my time serving three churches as paying my dues." The circuit-riding preacher making his or her rounds from small church to small church may have been the norm for a former generation of clergy, but it is not the way many of the current generation of ministers anticipate spending their lives.

As has been pointed out, the small congregation that is part of a multi-church parish is going to be a prominent part of Protestantism for the indefinite future. They have been and will continue to be feasible organizations for carrying on the Christian witness and ministry. In fact, one cannot study such churches without concluding that they are underrated as instruments for carrying on the Christian witness. This is true in spite of the fact that they may not fit the denomination's or the clergy's model of what a local church ought to be. In the small multi-church parishes, people do learn about the Christian faith. They witness to that faith and share it with others. And they support and care for one another and for other persons in the larger community, and contribute to the worldwide mission of the church.

It is important that both the laity and the clergy recognize that the multi-church parish is and will continue to be a feasible form of organization for the small congregation. One cannot study a large number of these churches without concluding that more effort sometimes seems to be going into attempting to make the congregations fit into some preconceived form or organization than in attempting to work creatively with them as they exist. They are vital institutions that have an important place in the lives of their members. They are a significant part of their denominations. They are not anachronistic institutions that have outlived their usefulness, but churches that can continue to witness and serve effectively. If the idea is accepted that churches of small membership which share a pastor with other congregations are going to be a significant part of Protestantism for the indefinite future, several things can be done to increase their effectiveness.

Toward More Effective Multi-Church Parishes

The church exists because of God's actions. Christian people adopt a particular life-style, engage in certain activities, and refrain from others because of what they believe. Basic to the church is the people's understanding of what God is calling them to be and to do at this time. The theological understanding of the nature and purpose of the church will determine both its organizational form and program. Every local church needs to have a clear understanding of who it is and what its purposes are.

The church is the people of God, but these people are also part of a larger society. The community of which the members are a part will have an impact on the local congregation, but it does not determine the purpose of the church. This is determined by the people's faith. How the congregation organizes itself and what activities it undertakes to achieve its purpose will to some extent be determined by the kind of community in which the people live. On one extreme will be the large city-church of several thousand members; on the other will be the rural church with a few dozen persons. Both may have the same purpose but will organize themselves differently to achieve it because the communities in which they serve are different.

If the congregation does not have an understanding of its nature and purpose, it will take its direction from the culture of which it is a part. It will be co-opted for various causes, which may or may not be consistent with the people's understanding of the Christian faith. The church is not primarily a lobbying group, a welfare agency, or a social action organization although at times it may contain elements of all three. It is the people of God in a given time and place who gather to worship, to witness, and to serve. Only by a clear theological understanding of its nature and mission can the church determine its own course, and act rather than only respond.

If the theology of the church is understood, whatever institutional form it utilizes will be seen as secondary. The institution will be perceived as a means to an end, not an end in itself. The validity of whatever form of organization is used will be tested by our asking if it is effectively enabling the church to achieve its goal. Such an understanding should reduce the invidious comparisons between different types of local churches, because all are means to a greater end.

Although theological clarity is important for every congregation, it is particularly important for multi-church parishes. This form of organization is a feasible method of carrying forward the mission of the church in certain types of communities. It is therefore as valid and important as any other type of parish structure. It is one way that the people of God who live in a particular type of community can organize themselves in order to have the services of an ordained minister and carry forward the work of the church.

A theological understanding of the church is necessary for

90

determining the criteria of success of a local congregation. Success or failure must be judged in light of the church's goals. Unless these goals are pinned to theology, success will be judged solely in regard to institutional development. Success will be measured primarily in membership growth, funds raised, property acquired, and programs carried out. Such activities are important, but they are hardly the only, or even the most important, measures of an effective church. They are not relevant to those many congregations which are part of a multi-church parish. Such churches may have limited potential for growth, with all the property they need and too few people to carry on extensive programs. It is important to remember that the church has been called not to be successful in the development of its institutions but to be faithful in its witness and to minister in whatever situation it may find itself.

The multi-church parish is an institutional form requiring that each local congregation see itself not in isolation, but as part of the larger community of the people of God. The fact that congregations must cooperate in working out the details of sharing a minister and arranging for the parish schedule is a visible and continuing reminder that they are members of a larger church and not an isolated local unit. All congregations are of course part of the church universal, but those which are part of a multi-church parish are made aware of this fact. They work with other groups so that the church's ministry might be carried on in several communities.

The multi-church parish requires close cooperation between the laity and clergy. This of course is necessary in any type of church, but it is particularly critical in congregations sharing a pastor. The lay members must assume more responsibility for the ministry of their church. The pastor must be willing to trust the laity to witness to their faith and enable them to carry forward the work of the church.

It is of course understood that having a clear understanding of the nature and purpose of the church or even the best of cooperation among congregations and between the clergy and the laity will not eliminate the many practical problems. The budget must still be raised even though it may require sacrificial giving by the small group of members. The schedule of worship services and other activities must be worked out in a satisfactory manner despite the distance between the churches. And obtaining a minister, particularly one who is enthusiastic about serving a multi-church parish, is not always an easy task.

However, a clear understanding of the theology of the church will set the institution in proper perspective. One type of congregation will not be seen as more important than another type. All will be perceived as the people of God gathered to witness and serve in the community in which they live. Because wide variations exist between communities, local churches respond with different types of organizations and activities. One form of institution should not be seen as better than another, only different. The question that should be asked is whether a particular organization and program is effective in achieving the church's goals in the community in which it is located at this point in time.

One cannot study the church without concluding that it is the institution through which God works. Despite shortcomings, which can be found in any social institution, the church bears witness to the truth of the Christian faith. The church is the people of God gathered to worship and organized to reach others with the Christian message and to serve in the community of which they are a part. The multi-church parish is and will continue to be one form of organization that enables the church to witness and minister in many communities across the land.

Suggested Readings

Anderson, James D., and Ezra Earl Jones. *Ministry of the Laity*. New York: Harper & Row, Publishers, 1985.

Carroll, Jackson W., ed. *Small Churches Are Beautiful*. New York: Harper & Row, Publishers, 1977.

Dudley, Carl S. *Making the Small Church Effective*. Nashville: Abingdon, 1978.

Hassinger, Edward W., John S. Holik, and J. Kenneth Benson. *The Rural Church: Learning from Three Decades of Change*. Nashville: Abingdon Press, 1988.

Judy, Marvin T. *The Cooperative Parish in Nonmetropolitan Areas*. Nashville/New York: Abingdon Press, 1967.

———. *The Parish Development Process*. Nashville/New York: Abingdon Press, 1973.

Madsen, Paul O. *The Small Church—Valid, Vital, Victorious*. Valley Forge, Pa.: Judson Press, 1975.

Quinn, Bernard. *The Small Rural Parish*. Washington, D.C.: Glenmary Research Center, 1980.

Ray, David R. *Small Churches Are the Right Size*. New York: Pilgrim Press, 1982.

Schaller, Lyle E. *The Small Church Is Different!* Nashville: Abingdon, 1982.

———. *The Pastor and the People*, rev. ed. Nashville: Abingdon Press, 1986.

Smith, Rockwell C. *Rural Ministry and the Changing Community*. Nashville/New York: Abingdon Press, 1971.

Surrey, Peter J. *The Small Town Church*. Nashville: Abingdon, 1982.

Thiessen, John C. *Pastoring the Smaller Church*. Grand Rapids: Zondervan, 1962.

Willimon, William H., and Robert L. Wilson. *Preaching and Worship in the Small Church*. Nashville: Abingdon, 1980.

Willimon, William H. *What's Right with the Church*. New York: Harper & Row, Publishers, 1985.